John Adair

Hints on the Culture of Ornamental Plants in Ireland

John Adair

Hints on the Culture of Ornamental Plants in Ireland

ISBN/EAN: 9783337322274

Printed in Europe, USA, Canada, Australia, Japan

Cover: Foto ©Andreas Hilbeck / pixelio.de

More available books at **www.hansebooks.com**

HINTS

ON THE

Culture of Ornamental Plants

IN

IRELAND.

BY

JOHN ADAIR, ESQ., A.M.,
BARRISTER-AT-LAW.

"Say not thou, what is the cause that the former days were better than these? for thou dost not inquire wisely concerning this."

THIRD EDITION.

DUBLIN:
E. PONSONBY, GRAFTON-ST.; W. M^cGEE, NASSAU-ST.
LONDON: SIMPKIN, MARSHALL, & Co.
EDINBURGH: ADAM AND CHARLES BLACK.
1878.

TO

HER GRACE THE DUCHESS OF MARLBOROUGH.

Madam,

Knowing that your Grace feels deep interest and takes active part in all that helps to the welfare and happiness of the People of Ireland, and much enjoys the subject about which I write, I gladly avail myself of the privilege, very kindly given to me, of

Dedicating this Book

TO YOUR GRACE.

PREFACE TO FIRST EDITION.

THE kind reception by the Legal Professions of a law book I published not long ago, on a very dry subject, allows me to hope that a little work on a fascinating one will experience equal kindness from the larger body to whom it is addressed. If the suggestions in the following pages meet public approval, I will feel happy to add such further information as limited experience and persevering experiment may enable me to offer.

JOHN ADAIR.

May, 1870.

PREFACE TO THIRD EDITION.

The increasing interest which everywhere appears about Ornamental Plants, and additional information I have obtained since I published the last edition of this little book—now some years out of print—lead me to hope that a new edition may help many readers in enjoyment of the loveliest of Ornamental Arts. I think that, at the coming Meeting of the British Association in Dublin, it may be useful to visitors, and especially to ladies, lovers of horticulture, and little aware how the various moist, mild climates of Ireland suit different plants, native and exotic. At one of the first of their meetings which I attended, I was asked by the late Dr. Gray, of the British Museum, and a few other eminent naturalists, to write for a contemplated British Fauna that part relating to the conchology of Ireland; and feeling it right to decline this tempting invitation, I brought to their Meeting of 1840 a little book in which in the interim I sketched about 400 varieties of our choicest shells, and noted the habitats of many of the rarest: and some of one little species which I dredged in L. Strangford, and were the first that were ever found in a living state in the kingdom, so attracted the attention of Professor Edward Forbes, and Sir William Jardine, that they, I believe with others of kindred tastes, came to Ireland to search, and were much pleased with what they found here. From that time, engrossing engagements, professional and domestic, for many years hindered me attending the annual meetings: and now I find the subjects of female education, and remunerative employment for women, taking a prominent place in the consideration of enlightened philanthropists; and ornamental gardening in its various branches seems to present a large field for such occupation.

At page 116 I refer to the special importance which the first Napoleon attributed to Music, for the attention of statesmen and other leaders of the public mind; and other men of great eminence have ranked a fine taste for gastronomy and culinary art amongst the most valuable endowments of philosophers.

Henrion de Pensey, premier President of the

Court of Cassation, and the magistrate of whom Roger Collard said regenerated France had most reason to be proud, expressed himself as follows to three most distinguished men of science, Laplace, Chaptal and Berthollet: "I regard the discovery of a dish as a far more interesting event than the discovery of a star, for we have always stars enough, but we can never have too many dishes; and I shall not regard the sciences as sufficiently honoured or adequately represented amongst us, until I see a cook in the first class of the Institute." The Duc d'Escar, grand maître d'hotel to Louis XVIII., who was a gastronome of the first water, died inconsolable at not having given his name to even one dish, whilst that of Béchamel was decorated with glory for *Veau à la Béchamel*, of which he was supposed to be, though not really, the inventor.

A late accomplished Earl of Dudley, speaking of a learned Baron of the Exchequer, says "He was a good man, sir, an excellent man; he had the best melted butter I ever tasted in my life:" and we read that liqueurs were invented to stimulate the appetite of Louis XIV., when flagging in old age, having been prodigious in his youth.

Ornaments for the dinner and supper table, otherwise

than as mere articles of food, have long commanded much attention. Madame de Sévigny describes a remarkable royal collation in a room hung with *jonquils;* and the Prince of letter-writers, Horace Walpole Earl of Orford, condescends to write about ornaments fashionable for dinner tables and desserts in his days.

"The last branch of our fashion into which the close observation of nature has been introduced is our desserts. Jellies, biscuits, sugar-plums, and creams, have long since given way to harlequins, gondoliers, Turks, Chinese, and shepherdesses, of Saxon China. But these, unconnected, and only seeming to wander among groves of curled paper and silk flowers, were soon discovered to be too insipid and unmeaning. By degrees, meadows of cattle, of the same brittle materials, spread themselves over the table; cottages rose in sugar, and temples in barley-sugar; pigmy Neptunes in cars of cockle-shells triumphed over oceans of looking-glass, or seas of silver tissue. Women of the first quality came home from Chevenix's laden with dolls and babies, not for their children, but their housekeeper. At last, even these puerile puppet-shows are sinking into disuse, and more manly ways of concluding our repasts are established. Gigantic figures succeed to pigmies;

and it is known that a celebrated confectioner (Lord Albermarle's)* complained that after having prepared a middle dish of gods and goddesses eighteen feet high, his lord would not cause the ceiling of his parlour to be demolished to facilitate their entrèe." "Imaginez vous," said he, "que milord n'a pas voulu faire ôter le plafond."

Though table ornaments and dainty dishes have long tried the skill of many an artist, as much seems now to be devoted to plants for adorning the tables and rooms of the rich, as in the last century was bestowed upon painted china and devices of spun sugar. This branch of our subject, or that which is called town gardening, would alone supply material for a Treatise; and daily something new attracts the amateur's attention. Even within the last few days I have been surprised by seeing varieties of *Camellia* in beautiful bloom in a conservatory off a landing in a dwelling-house in so central a part of Dublin as Harcourt-street. Here Mr. Cornwall

* Here I may mention, in reply to inquiries I have often read in public print—Who composed and who was the hero of the popular song Robin Adair? Lady Caroline Keppel, daughter of the second Earl of Albemarle, composed it, and Robert Adair, whom she afterwards married, and who was surgeon-general to King George the Third, and second son of Sir Robert Adair, who fought for King William at the Boyne, and died in College-green, Dublin, in 1745, was the hero.

grows about three score specimens of this very ornamental evergreen; of which many bear flower every winter, though each individual plant seems to take a year of rest without blooming.

For many years, the showy lily *Imatophyllum*, which blooms in winter and early spring, has thriven in my dwelling-house without conservatory; and in a sheltered area in front of the same house, in Mount-street, a plant of a small genus named *Charlwoodia*, which authorities call a beautiful stove plant, is now in vigorous health after living three years out of doors. It is about nine feet high, and is the first specimen which has ever been tried out all the year in this kingdom.

Amongst showy plants, whose fitness for our city life I believe I had the pleasure of being the first to prove, are some of the kindred genus *Cordyline*; and if the lovely twining under-shrub *Lapageria rosea*, which I again mention as called after the maiden name of the Empress Josephine, prove as hardy and fit for even town culture as recent experiments promise, I think I have many friends who would consider this little book worth publishing, were it only to invite special attention to these, and a few other plants not yet common amongst us.

I know many trade catalogues containing vast stores of information on every branch of horticulture, and properly written in a didactic style unsuitable to such a work as mine. And in trying to use a style somewhat popular, I trust what I write does not deserve the character sometimes given to popular science, as a superficial exposition of results by a writer who himself understands them imperfectly, to the intent that his hearers or readers may be able to talk or write about them without understanding them at all.

JOHN ADAIR.

65, Lr. Mount-street, Dublin,
March, 1878.

CONTENTS.

	Page
INTRODUCTION,	1
DIVISION OF SUBJECT,	7
DWELLING-HOUSES:	
Room Culture; under Glass, &c.,	9
Window and Balcony Gardening,	22
Gardening in Yards, Areas, &c.,	32
Table Ornaments,	38
TOWN GARDENING:	
City Squares, &c.,	41
ROCK GARDENING,	51
TREES AS STREET ORNAMENTS,	57
PLANTING ABOUT RAILWAY STATIONS, ETC.,	58
GROUNDS ABOUT CHURCHES, ETC.,	60
BOTANIC GARDENS,	60
PEOPLE'S PARKS AND GARDENS,	75
VILLAS,	78
DEMESNES, ETC.,	95
CONCLUDING OBSERVATIONS,	111
INDEX,	129

ON THE

CULTURE OF ORNAMENTAL PLANTS IN IRELAND.

INTRODUCTION.

FROM the dawn of civilization, Poets and Philosophers, inspired and uninspired, vie with each other in praise of Horticulture. Nearly three thousand years ago, Oriental Sovereigns took distant journeys to hear lectures on this and other subjects, from that gifted man who had "wisdom and understanding exceeding much, and largeness of heart even as the sand that is on the sea shore." The Queen of Sheba returned home from Jerusalem, convinced by what she there witnessed, that one-half of the greatness of his wisdom had not been told her. And in the account of King Solomon's knowledge, that of the vegetable world is prominently mentioned; when he spake of Trees, from the Cedar that is in Lebanon, even unto the hyssop that springeth out of the wall.

Homer celebrates the gardens of Alcinous at Phæacia—

> "Without the courts, and to the gates adjoin'd,
> A spacious garden lay, fenced all around,
> There grew luxuriant many a lofty tree.—
> And on the garden's verge extreme
> Flowers of all hues smiled all the year, arrang'd
> With neatest art judicious."

The terraced gardens of Semiramis at Babylon were celebrated by Diodorus and Josephus; and by Xenophon, those of Cyrus the younger, at Sardis, whose reply to Lysander, admiring their beauty and inquiring about their management, is recorded, "What do you think has made the varied productions of these gardens? the labour of my own hands." Theophrastus, a disciple of Aristotle, considered the habits of plants as worthy of study as those of man, bearing each to the other striking analogy—thus early teaching some leading doctrines on the subject, which are now commonly regarded as of modern discovery or invention. The Peach is mentioned by Confucius; and Almonds were sent from Canaan into Egypt to Joseph, as amongst the choicest fruits then known.

After the late Sir Thomas Staples, one of the longest survivors of the Irish House of Commons, had passed his eightieth year, I had the pleasure of teaching him, in his garden at Lissan, to bud roses and other ornamental plants, which he wished to learn, and afterwards practised; and on that occasion, as I best remember, he pointed out, in some life of Cicero, mention of the orator stealing out from Rome, in his busiest times, to a favourite villa, to watch the growth of his Oriental Plane trees.

I introduce the next few passages from the pen of Cicero, about other men of note, as somewhat showing the salutary influence of change from city to country, for however short a time, and of pretty plants and flowers, on minds which might be thought little susceptible of such impressions.

In his work on Oratory, Cicero describes a dialogue which was held under a tree of the Platanus group, which were some of the first exotics introduced into Italy for beauty. It was at a villa of his friend, Lucius Crassus. At a time of public tumult, Crassus retired from Rome, during the games there, to his Tusculan villa, as if, says Cicero, to collect his thoughts. He brought with him two promising students of oratory, for whose instruction the dialogue was introduced—Caius Amelius Cotta and Publius Sulpicius Rufus; Quintus Mutius Scœvola, an eminent lawyer and father-in-law of Crassus, and Marc Anthony, made up the party. The subject was taken from one of Plato's Dialogues, and, if worthy of the pens who wrote, may not be uninteresting to some readers of these pages, who have forgotten or been ignorant of it.

Phœdrus (meaning the beautiful or lovely), after a busy day in Athens, was going to refresh himself by a walk outside the city, when he meets Socrates, who says, "My dear Phœdrus, whence come you, and whither do you go?—From Lysias, son of Cephalus, to take a walk outside the city, for I have been sitting in the room since daybreak." Phædrus intimates that perhaps Socrates could not spare time to join him in his walk, to which the philosopher replies—" What, man! do you not think that, as Pindar says, if I had not leisure I should make it, to hear the result of your studies with Lysias?" And he tells him that he would not part him till he delivered the speech with which Lysias had regaled him, and which he was carrying in his mind, or probably under his cloak, intending to study it as he walked. Here they turn off the public road, and walk barefoot to cool themselves in the edge of the Ilissus, towards a lofty Plane tree which from a distance attracted their attention. Socrates, who seldom left the city, now apparently refreshed, says to his friend, " You have found the way to cure me of my home-keeping propensities. As men lead cattle onwards by holding food or fruit before their noses, so you lure me with the discourse you have in your book; and, for aught I know, you will lead me round Attica, or wherever you please. We have a pleasant retreat under this wide-spreading tree; shaded in by lovely shrubs, this place is full of the fragrance of herbs, and truly is most agreeable."

Were Ilissus' bank the inviting spot which imagination paints, we can't sit and converse there; nor can I, like Crassus or many of his contemporaries, entertain friends as I might wish to do in a villa on the banks of one of our neighbouring streams; but we all can enjoy our Botanic Gardens on the Tolka, at Glasnevin, where Addison, Swift, and Delany, and kindred spirits, spent many a classic hour in the grounds of their friend Tickell. And here, in addition to natural beauty, we have enjoyment which was not vouchsafed to ancient worthies, in the choicest trees and shrubs and flowers which each quarter of the world, vieing with the others, offers to the admiration of our days. And I dare to say that in such scenes the mind most highly and thoroughly schooled in science, and accustomed to abstract thought—

"—— with filial confidence inspired,
Can lift to Heaven an unpresumptuous eye,
And smiling say, My Father made them all."

Disclaiming any pretension to treat scientifically a subject on which the Press teems with works of that character, I invite the attention of readers of all ages and circumstances to varieties of interesting plants, from which selections may be made to please any taste. I particularly address my brethren of the working orders, for I believe never were such pursuits as ornamental gardening and kindred recreations so important as now to members of that class, on whom political and social powers are daily devolving. For members of religious orders, and vast numbers of other persons whom peculiar circumstances debar from many ordinary social enjoyments, our subject seems specially suited; and to clerics of all denominations it recommends itself as useful in promoting and fostering high and healthy tones of religious feeling. To women generally, on whom, from the Roman matron to our own aristocrat, artisan, or peasant, formation of character and happiness much depend, I commend this interesting recreation for their own personal enjoyment, and for judicious encouragement amongst youth. For man or woman foregoing till advanced years the pleasures of married life, with its attendant cares, the more to devote their vigorous years to some favourite pursuit, our subject is very valuable. Ornamental plants and flowers prove to be very useful in restoring minds overwrought and unstrung, and may reasonably be regarded as more salutary in preserving the mind in normal health and soundness. Now-a-days, when leaders of the public mind are puzzling themselves to discover remunerative employments for women and girls, is there not a large and pretty open field connected with different branches of ornamental gardening, and in some for which the female hand is much more gifted than the coarser hand of man?

I find in leading publications, not particularly given to write on the subject, cogent reasons for encouraging ornamental gardening amongst girls and women of all classes. I may refer to an article in *The Spectator* for the year 1876, page 686, recommending this employment to ladies, not only as highly conducive to health of body and mind, but as remunerative and capable of being made very profitable in various branches and ways, and expressing surprise that it is not oftener and more strongly than hitherto recommended for such purposes.

DIVISION OF SUBJECT.

Now I will offer some hints as to plants for growing in dwelling-houses, in glazed cases, or in the open room without such protection, and as to what is commonly called window-gardening. We will suggest some things which may be considered improvements in areas and yards, and places often miscalled town gardens; and in public squares, and grounds about churches, and in graveyards and cemeteries, in grounds at railway stations, &c. I will name some plants not so commonly known as they soon may be, for villa and other suburban ornament; and I will invite attention to the valuable schools which Botanic Gardens and peoples' parks and gardens are and may be to plant-growers and lovers of gardening. And before closing, we may glance at what is a-doing in cultivation of trees and shrubs, and other ornamental plants, on a large scale, in demesnes and private parks, of which there are noble examples in many parts of Ireland.

Here it may not be amiss to say a few words about what is called acclimating, which engages increasing attention as intercommunication of countries presents us with varieties of lovely plants till of late unknown amongst us. Artificial adaptation of foreign plants to circumstances different from those of their native home, trying to imitate in culture the treatment they experience in their wild state, seem to be important phases of acclimation; and much interesting work may be accomplished in this way without expecting to make any individual plant hardier here than it is in its indigenous state. Early, Lord Bacon foretold great improvements to arise from hybridizing of plants, by which means, and by what is called crossbreeding, offspring of rather tender parents prove themselves comparatively robust. Judicious choice of situation is particularly important; and for many plants a common mistake is often made in supposing that a close and sheltered spot is better than or as good as an open airy one.

Vast numbers of lovely exotics which suit our climate come from high tropical regions, and other high, dry, and airy situations; but many choice plants luxuriate in low, damp places, and the taste of each should be indulged. The natural season for a plant's chief beauty at its native home does not always correspond with ours, wherefore artificial aid may be lent, and due attention given to periods for excitement and for rest. In Dr. Hooker's work on Himalayan plants, and elsewhere, he notices, what might not be expected, some lovely stove plants as requiring much moist heat in summer, but comparatively cool treatment in winter.

It has been suggested to me to give a popular name to each plant I mention. I fain would do so, where the name is easily understood; but what think you of the name of a rather curious plant in its native country amongst the Astecs, *Macpalxochitlquahuitl*, meaning the hand-flower tree?

DWELLING-HOUSES.

Room Culture; under Glass, &c.—Whoever knows what disappointment till of late awaited every effort, even of persons in comfortable pecuniary circumstances, to have a constant supply of a few plants for ornament in the dwelling-house, can appreciate the changes in this direction which our generation has witnessed. Now we are so accustomed to see various plants flourish in closed cases, as almost to forget that our parents were unacquainted with such culture. And though what are called Ward-cases be but modifications of the cap-glass or conservatory, the honour of their introduction into society is attributed to Dr. Ward, who but recently died.

Amongst pretty little plants not often tried in such places as we now speak of, are varieties of the Piperomia group, with rather showy coreaceous leaves, which contrast well in a case with ferns. These are easily cultivated, and can be grown from single leaves with short leaf-stalk.

After continued failure of the horticulturist Loddiges in trying to grow the Killarney fern, *Trichomanes radicans*, the late Baron Fischer, superintendent of the Czar's botanical establishment at

St. Petersburg, being in England on a botanical tour, visited Doctor Ward in London. Surprised at the appearance of this fern (which the Baron had vainly attempted to cultivate), flourishing in a Ward-case apparently in untoward circumstances, the enthusiast took off his hat and bowed low to the plant, saying, " You have been my master all the days of my life!" Half a century ago Dr. Mackay, at our Trinity College Botanic Gardens, grew this fern out of doors in a pot plunged in a border covered with a cap-glass, perhaps little thinking how soon, if ever, it would flourish as it now does even in a garret in any of our cities. Still, whilst millions of plants are grown in rooms and windows, and a glazed case for the purpose may be made at a trifling cost, it seems surprising how few kinds we cultivate in this way, compared with what are within reach. In the autumn of the year 1872, some specimens of a spotted variety of what is commonly called the Arum lily, by name *Richardia*, in one of these cases outside a window in Piccadilly, attracted my attention as amongst the prettiest foliage plants I had seen in such circumstances. This lily is making its way into our houses and gardens, and roots may be purchased at small cost. I have seen two roots I planted in spring in flower-pots produce before autumn seventeen shoots and six flowers.

Filmy and other Ferns.—Different kinds of *Trichomanes*, and of its kindred *Hymenophyllum*, whose habitat is shady woods of the Tropics, and some of which abound in New Zealand and Madeira, and in the British Isles, seem gifted with a power of enjoying perpetual freshness even in the roomkeeper's humble abode. Their pellucid foliage has remarkable texture, which, long after vitality is lost, assumes on being immersed in water the appearance of vigorous life. I have had a glass-case some three feet long, and perhaps two feet broad, full of *Trichomanes radicans*, inside a window for several years, and in good health, without seeing a ray of sun. For months at a time it does not require to be freshly watered. The following mode of planting this fern was shown to me by the late Dr. Robert Smith of Dublin, who was long a very successful cultivator of native ferns there. Spread one or two inches of broken potsherd or cinder on the bottom of the box or pan in which the plants are to grow. If it be made of wood, line the bottom with zinc or lead, having holes in it for drainage. Over that layer of drainage another layer may be laid, of pieces of the fibrous outer shell of cocoa-nut; and on that again another layer of pieces a few inches in diameter, of a sod of common firm turf. On this scatter a little sandy peaty mould, keeping the surface pretty smooth, and water with a fine-rosed watering-pot. Then lay your fern down, and scatter a little more mould over the roots, and after sprinkling the plant with water close the case. These ferns are propagated in various ways, from division of the racemes with rootlets, and from young plants which grow from the sori or seedlets, which in favourable circumstances come in abundance along the edges of the fronds. Most ferns like rather shady situations and peaty mould, and when grown inside windows they may be moved back into the room in severe weather; and always suitable ventilation should be attended to.

Some peculiarly graceful and elegant kinds of the group called *Todea*, natives of South Africa, New Zealand, and New Holland, which have hitherto been costly and rather rare, are now imported in considerable numbers. *Todea pelucida* and *T. superba* are, amongst others, most generally known and admired; and whilst in their native wilds they attain a height of many feet, they are amongst us as pot plants in a young state, and quite gems of easy management. They seem to luxuriate in warm moisture and subdued light, but bear a cold or cool place and a dark situation. We see them in much beauty in pots standing in a few inches of water in a pan or saucer, covered with a glass-bell or frame, and daily sprinkled overhead. The *Gardener's Record* for August, 1876, page 549, quoting from *The Garden*, describes a flourishing plant, nearly filling a 24-inch bell-glass, in a room where it had been for four years. At the commencement of that time this plant, well named superb, was a tiny seedling, with but a couple of fronds scarcely one inch long, and at the close it had upwards of fifty healthy fronds, and meantime it produced some seedlings. It grows in a 3-inch pot, over whose edges rootlets ramble through Hypnum moss, which surround the little pot in a shallow seed-pan. Unsubdued sunrays are not allowed to strike upon the plant, which is watered as it seems proper, from once in ten days, or less, to once a-month.

Many other ferns have proved their aptitude for growing in rooms, and doubtless many more will do so than I can as yet vouch for; and the deep green and transparent surface of that which I have last described seems, as it were, covered with countless drops of dew like diamonds.

I might specify varieties of what we call Maiden's hair, *Adiantum;* also varieties of *Davallia, D. Moor-eana,* or *Moorei,* and others called hares-foot ferns; and of *Asplenium,* of each of which families there are many kinds.

Hymenophyllum is a genus of filmy fern, many of which are native to Chili and New Zealand, &c., and two kinds of which group, but a few inches high, are found abundantly in various parts of the British Isles. One of the prettiest cases of this plant I have seen was at a workman's show at Dundee, several years ago. These elegant plants like a particularly moist atmosphere, for which reason in rooms they are inclosed under glass.

Selaginellas, in some respects, resemble ferns. They are a genus of club-mosses; and of them, as of *Lycopodiums,* there is a great variety, many of which are very elegant in structure and habit. Most of these several kinds of plants are rather easy of culture, and may be abundantly increased by cuttings and division of the roots.

The ordinary soil for ferns, and plants of kindred nature, is sandy peat, but many thrive in other soils, fibrous loam, &c.; all require attention as to watering.

I know not any family of greater variety and attractiveness, of more extensive use, and found in more different climates, than Palms. In native wildness, and under costly culture, many become forest trees, whilst others are always small; but some of both characters are ready to enjoy a home in a dwelling-house, either under some kind of glass shade, or in an open room. Mr. Tyerman, when Curator of the Liverpool Botanic Gardens, showed me a plant of *Rhapis flabellata*, about twenty inches high, under a glass-bell in a living room, where it had been in good health for eight years. In the *Gardener's Chronicle* for the year 1872, page 730, amongst plants which were exhibited at a meeting of the Royal Horticultural Society of St. Petersburg, a fine specimen of *Areca Bauerii* is mentioned as having been three years in a room, and being many feet high. This Palm, and *Areca sapida*, from New Zealand, are ornamental in a young stage, and we will mention them again as amongst the hardiest of the family for trial out of doors. Sandy loam, somewhat enriched, suits these and many kindred plants.

Palms, &c.—Amongst Palms for room culture,

Corypha Australis is recommended, as are also varieties of *Chamædorea*, as *C. Hartwegii*, &c. *Phœnix dactylifera* may be grown in a room from the kernel of the fruit, which we have eaten.

Phœnix reclinata, *P. humilis*, *P. sylvestris*, *Cocos coronata*, and *C. flexuosa*, *Ptychosperma Cunninghami*, *Rhapis flabelliformis*, *Sabal Andansonii*, *S. umbraculifera*, *Seaforthia elegans*, *Thrinax elegans*, *T. radiata*, may be here named, amongst many.

I venture also to invite attention to varieties of *Cycacidæ*, which family form a link between the Palms and the Pine, and to which of late our amateurs seem for the first time to pay much attention. Many of these are ornamental in young stages, and easy of management, bearing considerable hardship, and not difficult to be procured. They like rather rich soil, and to have it sometimes judiciously watered with guano water or other liquid manure. I have known seedlings of one kind, *Encephalartos M‘Kenii* (I believe from Queensland), and of others, to stand throughout winter, near Dublin, in a cold frame. *Macrozamias* belong to the same family.

For amateurs with ample means and scanty room for indulging the taste, Nature has provided gems which occupy but small space, and amongst others many Orchids. One family of these little treasures, *Anœctochylus*, coming from Java and other hot countries, are terrestrial orchids, whose foliage, which is a net-work of pretty colours, is their chief beauty. The leaves of some varieties are traversed with fine golden and silver veins on purplish or rich green ground. It is well to nip off the flower-stem before it matures its bloom, for flowering so exhausts the plant as to endanger its damping off. With us these plants are generally grown in hot-houses, but men of experience think they are over-cooked, and that many species could be managed in a glazed frame in an ordinary room. The variety *A. setaceus*, from a coolish region of Ceylon, dislikes much heat, and probably others are congenial in this respect. The family in general like a sunny aspect, with partial shade from glaring sun. Some of these and kindred plants are figured in the fourth volume of Blume's *Flora Javæ*.

Sphagnum and sand form proper soil; and culture of these plants in rooms, as of Piperomias, abovementioned, seems to pleasingly contrast with that of Trichomanes and others of that group, so as to be worthy of remark. The Killarney fern has lived for years in a large, wide-mouthed bottle or glass jar, without water being once added to what it had when first inclosed, whilst some of those orchids of which we speak require constant attention. Some invalids, and other persons who enjoy such room ornaments, like the frequent occupation which the one kind of plants requires and affords, whilst there are many people who admire what need but little care, and who could not bestow anything like regular daily attention.

Liliaceous Plants.—Notwithstanding the long time

that Lilies have been amongst us, there is much room for experiment and improvement in their treatment, and many kinds may be domesticated. The *Gardener's Chronicle* for 1873 has a series of instructive articles on lily culture, and they speak of different soils for different groups. At p. 215, a cut is given of a pot of *L. auratum*, with one tuft, on which there were 225 flowers one season. Moist, boggy soil is recommended for what is called the Canadense section, amongst which are *L. parvum*, *L. puberulum*, &c., and for *Martagons*, *Tiger lilies*, *L. auratum*, &c., cool loam, and moist, peaty, and rather heavy soils.

L. auratum has grown well in towns, in large pots, with about two-thirds sandy loam and one of decayed cowdung, and abundant drainage. The bulb may be placed about half-way down in the pot, just covering it with soil, and occasionally adding more as the stem grows; and avoiding frost, let abundant air be given on fine days. The lancifolium lilies grow well in rather light soils, and so do the umbellatum and Thunbergianum sections, such as *L. longiflorum*, *L. candidum*. *L. Neilgherrense* is a fine autumn flowerer in the garden.

Lilies, when permitted, seem to live in constant state of growth, preferring open ground to confinement of pot culture, or that of a glass-case. However, most kinds, I believe, will bear careful potting when coming into bloom, and replanting out after flowering. Upon potting, water freely, and avoid sudden exposure on moving out of confinement.

The loveliest Japan lilies bear our climates in most places. The roots may be stored late in autumn, in a dry shed, or dry, cool cellar, protecting from frost; and during winter and early spring, a little water may be judiciously given occasionally, to prevent the bulbs becoming parched.

Amongst liliaceous plants few, except perhaps Hyacinths and the Narcissus tribe, have long been more general favourites for rooms than what is commonly called the Egyptian Arum, or trumpet lily. This handsome plant, more correctly called *Richardia Africana*, in compliment to an eminent French botanist, is a native of the Cape of Good Hope; and though I know it many years in the open ground and in ponds, in different parts of Ireland, blooming annually, it is generally cultivated indoors. About the year 1858, two, much smaller and more compact growing kinds, were introduced into England from Port Natal, one of which, if not both, will I expect ere long be well known amongst us. *Richardia albo-maculata* is that to which I allude, as much showier than the other, which is named *R. hastata*, and of which it is supposed by some botanists to be a sport. The leaf-stalk and leaf and the flower-stalk and flower of each of these ordinarily grow one foot and a few inches high. The leaf of *hastata* is variegated, and that of *R. albo-maculata* is spotted over with white spots. Its culture is very simple. Roots (which are cheap) may be planted in spring, and taken up in autumn, and kept in sand or other substance dry, till the time for replanting in spring. They increase freely and abundantly, and are easily divided. *Richardias* look well in or on moist edges of ponds or other waters; and I suppose the smaller kinds will grow out of doors permanently wherever the old larger kind thrives. I know of plants of the latter several years in a garden border, and others likewise in a pond. The spotted plant is well figured in the *Botanic Magazine* for the year 1859, tit. 5140, and in 13th vol. of *Flore des Serres* tit. 1343, where *R. hastata* also is described, whose flower is a greenish yellow.

Many of the lily group, and other bulbous-rooted plants, look well in beds or on swards carpeted with saxifrages or sedums.

At close of winter, and in early spring, a very showy lily, whose brilliant colour contrasts well with the white of *Richardias*, namely, *Imatophyllum*, or *Imantophyllum*, called from ιματος, of a strap, and φυλλον, a leaf, from its leaf being shaped like a leather strap, is as easy of cultivation in a dwelling-house as any plant. This I discovered as it were accidentally. About the year 1868, a large tuft of this plant, with several umbels of its bright orange-tinted vermilion flowers, particularly attracted my attention in a hot-house of my friend, the late Dr. Charles Croker, in Merrion-square. Considering it akin to *Clivea nobilis*, which we knew had lived healthily and bloomed freely in a rather exposed place in my dwelling-house, he gave me one or two roots, which have grown into several, living about seven months of the year in a room, flowering in March or April, and the other months plunged out of doors with *Richardias*, *Vallotas*, &c.

For rooms, halls, areas, and other places in and about houses in Dublin, and, I presume, in most parts of Ireland, the blue African lily, *Agapanthus umbellatus*, cannot be too strongly recommended. Every summer, for a quarter of a century out of doors in Dublin, it has sent its flower-stems well above its foliage, with trusses of bright blue blossom, in shape much like the *Imatophyllum*. This lily grows well in strong loam, with sand and leaf-mould rammed pretty tightly. *Imatophyllum* likes more pot room, with good, strong, rich soil. One variety is of somewhat deeper red than others, and more admired.

The Scarborough lily, with the varieties *Vallota purpurea*, *V. p. eximea*, and *V. p. major*, are a beautiful lily, and particularly well-adapted for greenhouse, frame, and window culture. They are not expensive, and increase freely.

Many kinds of bulbous-rooted and other liliaceous plants may be flowered under somewhat like treatment. *Scillas*, from the azure blue of Siberia to the bright tiny native of a few of our own hills, and some of creamy white, are a very pretty group. Small varieties suit well round hyacinths, tulips, and other bulbs in window boxes and other glazed cases, and in garden borders, with varieties of crocus.

Though Lily of the valley be native in some parts of this kingdom, it is charming when well-grown as a pot plant in rooms late in winter and in early spring; and for this purpose it is much cultivated in Holland and other parts of the Continent, and thence imported by us. Incipient flowering buds are easily distinguished from such as produce only leaves, and may be selected and grown with a view to potting. Water freely in summer, occasionally with liquid manure; pot in autumn; don't push or force your plants early, say, not before Christmas. There are different kinds, of which some are finer than others.

Aloes, and other Soft-wooded Plants.—For many years, what is commonly called the American Aloe, or Agave, has established its aptitude for room culture, flourishing there with less care than most plants require. It is of the Amaryllis tribe, and will live for many winter months without water to its roots, and it need never be watered overhead. Of late years, like qualities in other kindred plants have made them favourites for city culture—but it is well occasionally to water the soil. And some collections, of what are commonly called succulent plants (of which I may particularly notice that of Mr. J. T. Peacock, at Sudbury House, Hammersmith, near London) attract the admiration of many visitors, who are surprised at what can be grown in such seemingly unpropitious localities. Dr. Kellock, of Stamford-hill, Kingsland-road, London, has also a choice collection of soft-wooded plants, which have been chiefly cultivated by his own hand.

Aloe albo cincta, figured in the volume of *Botanical Magazine* for 1860, may be named as a handsome species, remarkable in foliage, and perhaps more so in its drooping flowers of rich yellowish-red colour.

Beschornerias form a small group akin to those last mentioned. *B. Yuccoides* is figured, &c., in the same volume of the book just now referred to; and several young seedlings have stood some winters well in Dublin in a frame at rere of my house. The flower is on a long, slender, coral-coloured scape and panacle, with gracefully stooping branches of the same colour; with racemes of pendent yellowish-green flowers, tinged with red, and shaped somewhat like those of some common fuchsia. *Beschornerias* are natives of Mexico, and are readily raised from seed, which is freely produced by plants which have reached the flowering stage.

Window and Balcony Gardening.—In towns and cities, culture of plants in the dwelling-house is particularly interesting, owing to the little space generally available there for out-door culture. Impediment to entrance of light and air to rooms is to be avoided; to which special regard should be had in the placing of frames or cases in window openings. Aspect also is to be considered; for many plants to which a sunny aspect is grateful soon show inability to prosper in any other, whilst there are as many which cannot endure direct and unsubdued sun-rays. Here observation and experience befriend us; and often a sunny aspect is desirable, but with partial shading, such as is given by gauze, or muslin, or paper, or otherwise. For above a hundred years from the first growing of bulbs in water in glasses, early in the seventeenth century, hyacinths and a few other bulbous-rooted lilies were the chief support of the amateur window-gardener. The simplest form of the gardening of which we now speak seems to be the growing of plants in pots or boxes, and these may be plunged in moss or cinders or some other substance immediately inside the window, or on the sill outside; and I believe much more can be in this way achieved than has yet been attempted.

Again, frames may extend from within the window to without the sill, thus having larger space for plants than where the frame is wholly in one of those places. I need scarcely suggest avoidance of draughts; and cleanliness, by sponging, syringing, or otherwise washing.

When the fireplace in the room is not required for its ordinary use, ornamental boxes, with the flower-pots inserted in moss, may take the place of the fender; and sometimes looking-glass is fitted in the open, where plants reflected have very good effect. Often of late we see the chimneypiece for a time devoted to plants in a growing state, as well as to cut flowers; and we need scarcely suggest that there are many other places in the dwelling-house, such as lobbies, &c., which may be turned to good account for like purposes.

I have seen in the centre or other part of a room a group of plants in pots, plunged in moss or sphagnum, and surrounded with basket-work, with very pleasing effect. Sods of living sedums or saxifrages, or sempervirens, &c., may well be substituted for moss, and without the same risk of turning brown.

Extending our work to window-balconies, we may find a much larger variety of suitable climbing and other ornamental plants than we are wont to see in such places. Here boxes may be used, with bottoms of tile, slate, or other durable material, and various pretty edgings are made with rustic and other moulding. Sometimes trellis of wire or wood, arching over a window, looks well, and the centre-piece may be movable. Boxes should be deep enough to hold six to nine or more inches of soil, and lead, slate, or zinc, may be used for lining. In this branch of gardening, provision for liberal watering is requisite—cistern, hose, syringe, &c., having each its own function. At times, many plants enjoy frequent dew-like sprinkling, but caution is necessary how this is done in bright sunshine, and escape for surplus water should be provided.

Here various climbers and other plants may be grown, some evergreen, some deciduous but perennial, and annuals; and of all, many stand out in places very near to others where they would quickly perish, and often from causes little anticipated. Our old favourite, *Pyracantha, Mespilus pyracantha*, needs no commendation; but *M. crenata*, and a few other varieties, are much prettier for fruit and foliage, and not generally so well-known as the other.

What is commonly called *Pyrus (Cydonia) Japonica*, of which there are several varieties, red, pink and white, are lovely late in winter or early spring, when well grown; and I believe a ripe fruit is useful in flavouring an apple-pie.

The shrub from which the public fancy that all which they call Tea is produced is of the Camellia family; and though not so ornamental as ordinary camellias, is worthy of culture, from its peculiar interest. Assam, and other parts of northern Asia, are, I believe, the only countries in which we know of the edible Tea shrub being found in a wild state, and whether it is indigenous there will perhaps long remain mysterious. At least six *species* of Thea are grown in Upper India, China and Japan, all of which are evergreens, with white or rose-coloured flower; but only one or two of these produce the infusion of which we drink. There are three well-known *varieties* which produce what we call Tea:— *T. Assamica, T. Bohea* and *T. viridis*; many botanists considering the two latter but varieties of *T. Assamica*, to which they give the honour of being the parent. Japanese tradition ascribes the introduction of the Tea plant into that country from China by a Bhuddist priest in the sixth century. Lately happening to be at Dunganstown, near Wicklow, I looked for a bush of *T. viridis*, which for years was known there in the nursery garden of the late Mr. Hodgens, but it had disappeared, with almost all his ornamental shrubs and trees, of which scarcely a vestige remains. I may again mention an experiment which Mr. André Leroy is making in his garden at Anjou with Thea viridis, of which he has some hundreds grafted on camellias.

Perhaps for readers fond of what is called scented tea, I may elsewhere name a few of the plants which are used in China for the purpose.

Not many years ago, *Lapageria rosea*—called after the Empress Josephine, whose maiden name was Rose de Lapagerie—was a stranger in this country; now it is everywhere admired as a lovely climber for the cold conservatory, and it has here ripened abundance of seed. We have three varieties, of which two are red, and the flowers of one are much larger than those of either of the others: the third is white, and scarcer than the others. They are natives of a cool climate in Chiloe; and specimens have been planted out in different places in England and Ireland, where it is hoped they will thrive, having already flowered well outside houses, with the roots growing within. Remarkable power of enduring coal and other smoke has been shown in the neighbourhood of copper-smelting furnaces in the south-western extremity of South America.

Berberidopsis corallina, from the forests of Valdivia, is another charming evergreen climber: of scandent habit and rapid growth, and nearly hardy, it lives out well in many places. Late in summer or in early autumn, profusion of small bunches of coral-coloured bloom, in size and shape like those of some of the more common of the Berbery group, make it when well-grown a very attractive object.

I know of but two places in this country where any attempt has been made to grow *Mandevilla suavcolens* permanently out of doors without further protection than a wall. In a sheltered nook against a garden wall of the classic villa at Templeogue, where Archbishop Magee wrote his work on The Atonement, a plant of this favourite climber has freely bloomed and seeded.

Some ten or more years ago the present owner, Mr. Roach, who has an interesting collection of plants, had this maudevilla in a conservatory. For years growing luxuriantly, it did not flower, till a stray branch made its way through a broken pane, and bloomed and ripened seed outside. From this hint he planted a seedling, which has given some of its peculiar long narrow pods, with seed, which I hope will help to encourage further experiment toward introducing into many suitable places this ornamental and fragrant climber.

Some Magnolias, particularly the well-known variety of *M. grandiflora* called Lord Exmouth's variety, would form a fine feature on many balconies, which they do wherever I have seen them tried. In most parts of Ireland they bloom profusely in autumn; and their large creamy-white flowers are very fragrant, contrasting well with the thick, dark-green foliage. This family, of which there are many varieties, like rather rich peaty soil with loam, but thrive without peat.

Forsythias, a small group, of modern introduction, of the privet family, well suit such places; and *F. suspensa*, which, like *F. viridissima*, has profusion of yellow bloom at close of winter, or very early in spring, is well worthy of attention, and quite hardy. Though deciduous, these plants in mild winters have not long lost their deep green foliage of the previous year before the flower begins to show itself afresh.

Fortune's Japanese Jassamine. *Jasminum nudiflorum* is amongst the showiest winter-bloomers, expanding bright yellow flowers along its leafless branches, from December to February, despite of frost and snow; and this and others of the group grow well in smoky cities.

The golden-veined leaves and fragrant flowers of the Japan Honeysuckle, *Lonicera brachypoda aureo reticulata*, make it a general favourite; and *L. fuchsioides*, with bunches of scarlet bloom; and *L. Ledebourii*, with deep-red blossom, are, amongst others, well worthy of attention.

I may name some varieties of Ceanothus, so called from the colour of their flower, κυανος, blue or azure, *C. rigidus* from California, *C. dentatus*; *C. intermedius*, &c. *Clianthus magnificus* and *C. puniceus* are beautiful shrubs for walls or trellis; and *C. Dampierii*, whose flower is more remarkable than that of the others, has as yet not been skilfully treated in most places; but I do not know of its wintering out anywhere in this country, nor do I expect that it will do so.

Cotoneasters, of which several are evergreen, are invaluable for verandahs, as well as walls, and trellis, and rockery. *C. microphylla*, *C. Hookeri*, *C. Simmondsii*, *C. velutinus*, &c., are amongst the best known.

Even in our cities we may hope soon to see some kinds of Palms in many places; and seedlings and seed of the hardier species are coming within reach of most of us as to price; though as yet but few persons have given fair trial to any of this family as out-door ornaments, either in country or town.

Of *Chamærops excelsa*, *C. Fortuni*, *C. humilis*, *C. Martiana*, *C. Griffithiana*, *Jubæa spectabilis*, *Areca sapida*, *A. Baueri*, and of the recently-introduced *Pritchardi filicina*, I suggest fair trial out of doors, with slight protection according to situation and strength of plant, and other circumstances. *Areca sapida*, the Southern Betel Nut Palm, is an ornamental plant, and I believe the most southerly representative of the family, occurring so far south as 38° 22′; and by some botanists considered identical with *A. Baueri* of Norfolk Island. It is abundant in mountain regions, in the middle island of New Zealand, growing about seven feet high, where the natives eat the young inflorescence, calling the plant Nikau.

Chamærops Martiana ascends the Western Himalayas to about 8000 feet elevation; and growing to a height of about 40 feet, has much of its fronds annually covered with snow. I believe *C. Griffithiana*, or Pritchiana, is a small creeping species, found in masses high on barren hills of Afganistan and Beloochistan.

Of deciduous perennials, that commonly called five-fingerd Ivy, or Virginian creeper, *Ampelopsis hederacea*, is especially suited for balconies. The species or variety named *Veitchii*, or *Roylii*, or *tricuspidata*, from Japan, is of much more compact habit than our old acquaintance. It clings to walls or trees with tenacity, I believe, exceeding that of Ivy; and its green foliage of summer changes early in Autumn to rich purplish-brown crimson, retaining this foliage much later than the American plant. They grow in ordinary garden soil, and are readily increased from layers or cuttings.

Bignonia radicans and *B. grandiflora* are handsome climbers, with large bunches of orange bloom, and will bear our winters in many more places than have tried them. I have seen Bignonias very showy in the southerly parts of England and Ireland; and I particularly admired some in the gardens of M. Alexandre Behas' Hotel du Parc at Lugano. Somewhat resembling these, but on a smaller scale of foliage and flower, Eccremocarpus has been long admired in

Ireland, and intermixes well with other plants of scandent habit. These produce and grow from seed abundantly.

Wistaria sinensis, with profuse bloom like Laburnam in form, and of lilac color, covers almost any amount of surface; and a considerable continuance of flowering may be had by training some branches at the sunny and others at the shady side of a wall.

Everyone is acquainted with Clematis, of which lately new varieties greet us yearly. Some, amongst many which have been sent out by Mr. Jackman, are becoming as well known as the old sweet-scented species. Isaac Anderson Henry, Esq., has, amongst many gifts to the garden, raised fine seedlings of this showy group.

In many places Vines may be grown with the roots outside the house, and the branches either there or brought within the room; and each of us can form our own opinion how well-grown clusters of grapes look there, from their first forming till dropping with ripeness.

Several varieties of *Ipomœa*, Convolvulus, are very ornamental, amongst which may be named that which produces jalap.

I need not specially name any of the numerous annuals which may decorate such places as we have been speaking of.

Here I may notice a plan of conservatory, simple when suggested, but I believe not often seen. In the *Gardener's Chronicle* for the year 1876, p. 330,

Mr. Cox, of Mill Hill, N.W., on the Midland Railway, describes one recently made. On an outside wall of his drawing-room, in the centre of which are the chimney and fire-place, he has built a conservatory, with heating apparatus. For a large portion of the wall, at each side of the fire-place, he substituted plate glass, and in this building he keeps orchids and some congenial plants for a few weeks of their bloom; and he names about sixty of these giving a blaze of beauty at the time he writes. At first he feared that moisture condensing on the glass would obscure the view from the sitting-room; but he says that happily this does not occur, and that the partition glass has never been dimmed by damp. Plants are on brackets at different heights, and Dendrobes are suspended from the roof. *Phalænopsids* require to be removed to their ordinary abode after about two weeks' sojourn in the new house. *Odontoglossums* and *Oncidiums* preserve their health for four weeks or longer, seemingly benefited by the clime.

Gardening in Yards, Areas, Railway Stations, &c.—Having seen some advances which room and window-balcony culture have of late made, let us glance at a few improvements which seem easily attainable in such places as town yards, areas, and gardens, and other small patches of ground belonging to city, town, and suburban dwellings. Finding such ferns as *Trichomanes*, *Todea*, and *Hymenophillum*, &c., thrive even in garrets in dark parts of a city, may we not expect that many kinds of fern and other pretty plants will suit such places as we now refer to? In them, in glazed frames, from the simplest kind, composed of a box without bottom and a pane of coarse glass as a top, to an orchid palace, of which one is described above, for preserving within view of the sitting-room choice exotics during their greatest beauty, may be permanently grown or temporarily kept vast numbers of plants of various kinds as yet untried in such places. Glazed frames can readily be made to be taken asunder; and the less hardy Yuccas, and many of the soft-wooded families, *Aloes*, some *Agaves*, &c., thrive perhaps better where only the top is glass and the sides wire-work, than with the closeness of ordinary frames.

For encouragement in overcoming difficulties in such places as we now speak of, we may look to or read of the devices to which the Japanese had recourse before the use of glass was known in their gardening. We learn something of this in Mr. Fortune's work on Japan.

My late friends, Dr. Robert Smith, of Eccles-street, and Mr. Robert Callwell, of Herbert-place, made the first good collections of native ferns which I have known in Dublin. Dr. Smith, who was a very learned and eminent man in his own profession, commenced his collection many years ago, and from time to time as it increased he had recourse to various contrivances in his dwelling-house and small garden at its rere. And he so admired the Killarney fern, *Trichomanes*, that, in addition to many small cases of it which grew under glass in his garden, he devoted a stable loft to the same favourite, which he surrounded with boxes of this fern, with tops or fronts of glass.

Mr. Callwell had but few specimens of this fern; but one of these filled a glass-case some four feet long by nearly as many wide, which stood on a lobby in his dwelling-house, and which was so admired by Dr. Ward, of Wardian-case celebrity, that he seriously asked Mr. C. if he would take £250 for it. Half the garden Mr. Callwell covered with glass, and made of it a rock-work fernery, which was very successful.

Amongst foreign ferns, hardy, and nearly so, for trial in such places, I name *Woodwardia radicans, Cyrtomium falcatum, Onychium Japonicum*, of which latter the crowns may sometimes require slight protection, as by dried leaves, or turf-mould, or otherwise; *Pteris scaberula*, and others of the genus. *P. cretica albo-lineata* stands out in different places. *Gymnogramma Japonica, Lomaria Magellanica*, and *L. Chilensis*, whose fronds are sometimes three feet long. *Onoclea sensibilis*, which luxuriating in moisture may be well grown in damp places. *Struthiopteris Germanica*, with fronds three feet long; *S. Pennsylvanica, S. Japonica, Polysticum acrosticoides*, and others.

There are numbers of stables in and about our cities and towns where a horse is not kept, and of which little if any use is made, some of which might readily be transformed into conservatory or hot-house, and place for a gardener to work, and even to reside in. Some few stable-lofts in Dublin have for years been the gardener's abode, and parts of one stable have been converted into places for propagating and growing plants. I do not know of one here as yet being roofed with glass; but I have been in a hotel in Princes-street, Edinburgh, whose roof is glass, where vines ripen grapes; and a like plan has been adopted in America and elsewhere.

A few more plants may be mentioned, of which I have not known many in any of the places we now speak of, which I hope to see succeeding there—varieties of *Aloes* and other soft-wooded plants, with winter and spring covering overhead, and it may be quite open, or with wire-work around. The common *Agave*, called *A. Americana*, or *American Aloe*, has stood out many years in different parts of Ireland without covering. Likewise *Yuccas*, such as *Y. alowfolia*, green and variegated; *Y. treculeana*, *Y. filamentosa*, green and variegated; *Y. stricta*, *Y. albospica*, *Y. Whiplii*, *Y. angustifolia*, &c. *Cordylines*, *C. Australis*, *C. Banksii*, *C. indivisa*, &c.; *Begonias*, tuberous-rooted, which are again mentioned below, and other kinds.

Varieties of *Acanthus*, and of *Saxifrage*, too many to name here.

Of *Lilies*, as to which I may say the same.

Lily of the Valley, of which there are varieties better than others, though shade-loving, grows well in a southerly aspect. It may be enriched with well-decayed manure, and abundantly watered in dry weather. The proportion of bloom to leaf may be increased by removing leaf-shoots when young, which can readily be distinguished from those for flowering.

Rhododendrons, of which there are varieties of colour and hue, from pure white to deep crimson, and for which there are different seasons of blooming, from mid-winter to summer and autumn, and of which some are fragrant and some scentless, and some of stiff and others of scandent habit.

Privets, evergreen, as *Ligustrum coreaceum*; or nearly so, as *L. Japonicum*, *L. ovatum*, &c.

To *Skimmea Japonica*, *S. Laureola*, *S. oblata*, and *S. fragrans*, I particularly invite attention. Some come from mountains near Nangasaki, having small bunches of flower in March and April, in shape and colour somewhat like *Privets*, with sweet perfume, and with bunches of blood-red berries from summer till the following spring.

Several of the Myrtle and myrtaceous groups thrive in Dublin; and besides the common kinds, *Eugenia apiculata* has grown well in a sheltered border of Merrion-square, flowering for some months in summer. *Eugenia ugni*, and others, are in probation in our city.

But of all shrubs with evergreen or persistent foliage, varieties of *Aucuba* seem to me to receive more general admiration, proving themselves fitter for areas and yards of our cities than any other that I know of. Of these there are several, differing considerably from one another in size, shape, and colour of foliage, and of fruit. One variety, *A. Himalaica*, is described by Sir J. D. Hooker as delighting in humid spots, where mosses and lichens hang from the branches.

Judicious observation as to light and shade, eddies and currents of wind, &c., is specially important in selecting plants, and giving protection in confined areas, yards, and small gardens. Difference of a few feet one way or another may cause a plant to live or die. In September, 1867, I planted, in the small garden at the rere of my house in Dublin, two of the first *Griselinias* (a shrub nearly allied to *Aucuba*) I had seen. One I placed in what I considered the best spot there for the purpose, as sheltered and having early sun; the other I placed in what proved to be a well-sheltered spot facing westward. Some currents of wind, unexpectedly playing on the first of those plants, bent and scathed it before springtime, and the other was vigorous after more than twelve years, in the place where I doubted whether it would survive one winter. The only other kind of this evergreen I know, *G. macrophylla*, is much more showy, but much more tender, than *G. littoralis* above-mentioned.

In a little work, named *East and West*, whose preface is from the pen of the Countess Spencer, interesting mention is made of the beneficial influence of room and window culture of plants in parts of Eastern London, dark in more than one sense.

In an article in *Macmillan's Magazine* for 1873, entitled "Flowers for the Poor," the writer, sister of the Dean of Westminster, invites assistance in what she calls this "new missionary work in London," promising to make good use of contributions of flowers, and of suggestions toward extending the work already pretty largely in operation. It is very gratifying to witness, as I have done, much good fruit from this work in the neighbourhood of Westminster; and I could name men most eminent in their respective walks in life—with some of whom I have the pleasure and honour of being acquainted—who largely contribute to its advance.

Table Ornaments.—It seems not out of place here to mention table ornaments. Ever since plants have taken a prominent place in ornamenting the festive board, citizens find it far from easy to obtain such supply as they desire. For periodic display, where

> "Beggar pride defrauds her daily cheer
> To boast one splendid banquet once a year,"

a few ornaments may be procured; but it is another matter to have pretty plants always ready to pop upon our table for daily enjoyment. Though *bloom* be transient, it was long more valued for such purposes than beauty of foliage, which now assumes its befitting place.

Let us look at a few plants easy of culture, whose

flower is their principal ornament, and then at some of which foliage is their chief attraction.

Daily arrivals add to countless hot-house and conservatory beauties of established character, to which acres of glass would not do justice; and no one has ventured to limit the numbers which are within reach of persons of even small circumstances, and which are manageable with contracted resources. The lovely novelties which our day has witnessed from Japan call for especial gratitude to that interesting country, whose unexampled advances attract the attention of all Christendom.

For more than a century Hyacinths' brilliant colours, luscious fragrance, and facility of growth, have made them general favourites for rooms. *Tulips, Ranunculi, Jonquils, Narcissus*, and somewhat homogeneous plants, have also long sustained high repute; and a good specimen of any of these is worthy of a place on the table which entertains the noblest guests. Many other plants of comparatively recent introduction make beautiful table ornaments. Some *Acacias*, such as *A. lophantha*, *A. Drummondi*, &c., are easily procured and easily grown, and quickly make handsome specimens, either with or without their bloom. The reader may be reminded of the following, amongst infinite other table plants: *Roses, Heaths, Epacris, Rhododendrons, Orchids*, of which latter perhaps there is as great variety as of any known plant; some, and beautiful kinds, requiring little or no artificial heat beyond inclosure under glass; *Carnations, Pinks, Picottees, Veronicas, Lilies, Pelargoniums, Gloxinias, Agaves, Aloes, Anthuriums, Begonias, Caladiums, Camellias, Crotons, Dracænas, Genistas,* many of the Myrtle, and even some of the Pine group, *Thujas, T. Donneana,* &c. *Cryptomeria elegans* and others, *Cypresses,* and many other shrubs and forest trees in a young stage, and of some of which there are varieties which grow but small, are as pleasing to some eyes as table plants as are young palms or young tree ferns.

Of plants intermediate between those cultivated solely for the flower, and those whose beauty is foliage, ornamental berries, or fruit, have of late procured an introduction into society for some which have become prime favourites. Amongst these already mentioned, *Aucubas* are prominent. *Skimmeas,* also mentioned above; and though somewhat like *Aucubas,* they reach a height of several feet, they are whilst in a young stage handsome table ornaments. Bunches of scarlet fruit, which hold on till that of the next year is formed, contrast well with dark lance-leaved foliage. I see no reason why *Cotoneasters,* such as *C. Simondsii* and *Hookerii,* &c., which are very handsome shrubs when well pruned into shape, should not make nice pot plants for table ornament.

These now named are readily increased by cuttings, layers, seed, &c., and ordinary good garden soil suits them well. Besides these *hardy* berried plants, there are a greater variety of green-house and stove plants with ornamental berry or fruit than I am acquainted with. Some of our ordinary fruit trees likewise, peaches, nectarines, plums, and grapes, look well and delicious as table ornaments in flower-pots in a growing state.

But perhaps the most ornamental table plants appear there without fruit or flower. The impression made on me several years ago by two native ferns which, being taken from a ditch at Malahide Castle, where they were growing, and being put into white biscuit china vases ornamented the dinner-table in the venerable oak-room, and were the first of the kind I had seen, will ever be very pleasing.

TOWN GARDENING.

City Squares, &c.—In considering improvements to which we may look forward in what is called Town-gardening, town and city squares, and such places, may be regarded as fair ground for experiment.

Thirty years ago and earlier, when residing in Mountjoy-square, I sometimes asked an experienced foreman at Glasnevin gardens would this or that plant succeed in the city. "Try," he would reply; "little is yet known of town-gardening: but don't hope that they will thrive there without as good soil and care as they require in the country." With but little money to expend or time to bestow on such matters, I made occasional experiments, sufficient to warrant me to persevere, and encourage others to do so; and already I have enjoyed many a plant grown within our city bounds, and even within the influence of its smoke, which I would scarcely have ventured to try out of doors in those earlier days. I need not remind anyone who knows Dublin, that the circumstances, and I may say climates, of Fitzwilliam and Rutland and Mountjoy-squares materially differ each from the others, with respect to the growing of many plants. Hitherto our squares have not had proper staff or other provision for having them at all as ornamental as they may be. However, considerable improvement has been made in some of them since I first took an interest in Mountjoy-square, where I lived for over quarter of a century. Soon after entering manhood, very peculiar circumstances led me to take part in the improvement of that Square. Then two or three starved Hollies were its chief evergreen shrubs, with perhaps a few Aucubas, and the numbers have increased a hundredfold in that, and in Merrion and Fitzwilliam-squares.

Of Evergreens and plants with permanent foliage, many hybrid Hollies, remarkable for both foliage and berry, and worthy of particular attention, have of late been planted in some of our Squares. Also *Ilex Dipyrena, I. crenata, I. furcata, I. Fortuni, I. Tarago,* and *I. cornuta,* all of peculiar shape of leaf, promise to succeed in our towns, and some of them are doing well in Merrion-square. The latter variety is figured in Curtis' *Botanic Magazine* for the year 1858, Tab. 5059. And of these, as well as of the kinds with which we are more familiar, new and interesting hybrids and cross-bred kinds may be expected from time to time to appear amongst us. I made two unsuccessful attempts to grow *I. latifolia* in Dublin; and I do not remember having seen in culture the somewhat similar splendid Holly which is described in the 39th vol. of *The Botanic Magazine*, Tab. 5597, from the Sikkim Himalayas.

Of Yuccas, different varieties, such as *Y. recurva*, *Y. gloriosa*, *Y. flaccida*, flowering again and again in the same Square, proves their fitness for such places. I believe any of the variegated kinds, all of which are much admired, had not been tried out a whole year in any other of our large cities or towns till I lately made an experiment with a pretty strong plant, covering it overhead for winter. This is the filamentous species; and for some years, the Rev. Henry Ellacombe has grown rather large specimens of the variegated Aloe-leaved species close to a wall, against which he fastens a board at close of autumn above each plant, to protect it from rain, &c.

Almost all one number of Mr. W. Saunders' *Refugium Botanicum* is devoted to descriptions by Mr. J. G. Baker, and figures of different Yuccas; and the same pen has elaborately described, in *The Gardener's Chronicle* for 1870-1, all the species, and I believe varieties then known in cultivation. *Y. canaliculata* and others are figured in *The Botanic Magazine*. See Tab. 5201.

Several New Zealand Cordylines, by some called *Dracænopsis*, promise to follow Yuccas as ornaments, very peculiar in appearance, for our squares and other town gardens. One of the first of the group I noticed permanently out of doors I moved, in the year 1867, from the garden of my friend Major Bailie, on a bank of Lough Strangford, to my own in Dublin, and finding it stand out winters here, I planted it in a border of Merrion-square, where I hope it will long flourish. The only protection it has received has been sometimes drawing its long foliage up together in winter, and tying a soft string round it.

In summer, 1876, another friend, Fletcher Moore, Esq., gave me a plant of *Charlwoodia*, or *Cordyline Australis*, which had been with him for above a year out of doors and uncovered, and has continued so with me ever since. Cuttings strike readily of pieces of the stem, in sandy loam with peat or leaf mould.

Griselinia lucida, or *litoralis*, already mentioned, one of a small family allied to Aucubas, has thriven out in Dublin for several years. *G. macrophylla* is a much showier shrub, but it seems to require shelter in winter in most parts of Ireland, though it has lived, and well, out in favoured places without complete covering. It has wintered out at Sir F. Brady's, at Dalkey, not far from Dublin, and elsewhere.

Escallonea macrantha, named in honour of a Spanish traveller, is a lovely evergreen shrub, and promises to be valuable in town gardens for foliage as well as flower. There are several kinds of this family, which is allied to the Gooseberry, and native of South America.

One or more varieties of the Olive group, to which *Osmanthus* is akin, may likewise be expected to suit our town gardens, and are handsome evergreens.

Rhaphiolepis ovata, or Japonica, with thick, ovate, leathery leaf, and small bunches of white, sweetish flower, is another native of Japan which thrives in our towns.

There are several kinds of *Pittosporum*, natives of Australia, Madeira, Japan, Cape of Good Hope, &c. The New Zealanders call their plants *Karo*; one variety, *crassifolium*, is not an uncommon small tree in the Northern Island, and is recommended for extensive planting in the different islands, from its hardihood, and power to resist and bear sea winds. See *Flores des Serres* for April, 1875, p. 13. *Bot. Mag.*, Tab. 5978, A. D. 1872. It is said to require protection of a wall in eastern England, but it seems pretty hardy in different places near Dublin, and has been out for about two years in Merrion-square. It grows from four to ten feet high, dense and ramous, with erect branches, and leaves clothed underneath with white or buff. The flowers are generally in nodding umbels, small, dark, chocolate purple, and it seeds freely.

P. tobira is the species hitherto best known in Ireland, in many parts of which it grows out of doors. For twenty years it has been an ornamental shrub in Merrion-square, flowering freely every year about

June, and sometimes again early in autumn. The bloom, in shape, fragrance, and general appearance, resembles that of *Daphne odora*, but is not so fragrant.

P. coreaceum much resembles the kind last mentioned, and is scarce.

For the last few winters we have ventured to leave uncovered in a border of Merrion-square a specimen of *Chamærops humilis*, and now, in the winter of 1877, it looks healthy and promising. The last one or two years I have tried how another of these Palms will likewise fare in the garden at rere of my own dwelling-house, and I intend to give similar trial to one or more other kinds of hardy Palms.

I venture to suggest further trial of varieties of the Myrtle group, in parts of our cities and towns than has yet been given to these favourite evergreens. Amongst them I may name *Eugenia ugni*, from Southern Chili, whose fruit is eaten at dessert in its native countries. Another variety, *E. apiculata*, is figured in *The Botanical Magazine* for 1858, Tab. 5040. *E. luma* is one of the prettiest of these Myrtles, and bears our climates in many places. *Eugenia*, or *Myrtus clequen*, or *cleken*, of which a figure is given in *The Botanical Magazine*, Tab. 5644, has small oval leaves, about the size of those of our common garden Box, and, like some other kinds, well suits walls in many parts of the kingdom, though it sometimes suffers in severe winter seasons, or is burned by long summer drought.

Recently, fascination of what are called bedding plants, with brilliant bloom and foliage, becoming epidemic, seemed to threaten permanently to displace many herbaceous favourites from the prominence they long enjoyed as border plants, but reaction has set in in favour of intermingling the latter with the others, without injuring the claims of either. Even the limited opportunities I have had for observing how some handsome herbaceous plants, hitherto little tried in Dublin, will there succeed, encourage me to expect to see many growing luxuriantly amongst us.

We all remember varieties of *Saxifragia*, called London Pride and Paris Pride, as familiar to us in childhood. Now, at least one hundred and fifty kinds of this family are in culture, of which many beautiful varieties grow well in our cities. Large, fleshy-leaved species, such as *S. cordifolia*, *S. crassifolia*, are quite hardy, and have abundant bunches of handsome pink flowers in early spring, and some even before close of winter. *S. ciliata* is handsome, but not quite so hardy as those others. Several kinds, with slender flower-stems, varying in height from a few inches to about two feet, and of whose flowers some are white and others speckled and spotted, and with variety of foliage, come in later than the fleshy-leaved kinds, and are worthy of more general attention than they have hitherto received. *S. Nepalensis*, *S. Fortuni*, *S. ligulata*, *S. rosularis*, *S. pyramidalis*, &c., may also be mentioned. Some of the low-growing kinds form good carpeting, as it were, in which Lilies and other bulbous-rooted plants look better than growing in the clay-coloured bed.

Hellebores are particularly interesting as early bloomers. Long enough the common Christmas Rose was spoken of as if unique of its genus, now *H. atrorubens*, *H. atropurpureus*, and others, are pretty common. I specially notice *H. argutifolius*, or the Holly-leaved Helebore, as, to me, the handsomest of the family, and one which I have seen but in few places. It is well worthy of a conspicuous position for its foliage, irrespective of its handsome bloom. All, I believe, grow freely from self-sown seed, and in ordinary good soil.

Nasturtiums, Tropæolums, have gained a position in town gardening from which they are not likely to be displaced; but *T. polyphyllum*, which is, to my eye, one of the most interesting, I have not yet seen grown in any town, though I see no reason why it should not there succeed. Like most of the family, it is native of South America, and grows in racemes several feet long, radiating from a centre, and with yellow flowers and leaves thick along each. It is readily propagated by bulbs, which form deep below the surface; and the plant possesses a quality, like *Dictamnus fraxinella*, of generating and emitting in certain states of the atmosphere, towards evening, an inflammable gas and electric sparks, which was, I believe, first observed by a daughter of Linnæus. It flowers with much beauty at Glasnevin. See *Botanical Magazine*, A. D. 1869, Tab. 4042.

Foliage of many of what are called umbelliferous plants is particularly ornamental in young stages of growth. Amongst which are *Ferula communis, F. persica, F. tingitana, Oreocome filicina, Ligusticum Pelaponnesianum, Peucedanum officinale,* &c.

For more than twelve years, one plant of the common Heliotrope has lived in a border of Merrion-square, losing the foliage at close of autumn, and springing up before the next summer. Here also *Melianthus major* grows vigorously, though I have not known it to flower so far within the city. It likes light, rich soil and sandy loam, with which lime rubbish may be mixed.

Any kind of *Erythrina*, commonly called coral trees, is scarcely known in outdoor culture in Ireland, though some varieties are very suitable, and very showy. Natives of the tropics of both hemispheres, some of them attain a height of one hundred feet, with large dimensions; but grown in Ireland as a garden shrub, they die, or are cut down each autumn, to send up vigorous stems in spring, producing handsome blood-red, pea-shaped flowers, of various hues. *E. amasisa*, of Peru, is described as one of the most beautiful trees of the country, clad in spring and autumn with large flame-coloured vermilion bloom. Thirty years ago, I saw *E. crista-galli* flowering in Kingstown, near Dublin, where the only protection given was cinder or turf-mould at commencement of winter. This variety has been out many years in our College Botanic Gardens;

and at Mr. Veitche's Nursery, at Chelsea, I have seen it in a sheltered nook, where it has grown for some quarter of a century, flowering abundantly about August. *E. herbacea* is also well worthy of attention.

From the numbers of these plants which I saw for sale in nursery gardens on the Continent, particularly at Marseilles, at low prices, and the facility of growing them from seed and cuttings, no ordinary flower-garden need long be without one.

I may also suggest for such places varieties of *Lilies* and liliaceous plants, of *Acanthus* and *Saxifrage*, and *Anemones*, of *Campanula*, of *Mimulus*, and *Primroses*, and *Gentians*, of *Gladiolus*, and *Dahlia*. And for late autumn, approaching winter, *Chrysanthemums* are invaluable, as are *Hellebores* and *Christmas Roses*, of which now there are many kinds amongst us, for the close of winter and entrance of spring. Already the Japan primroses, whose introduction into this country made quite a sensation in the gardening world, are in tens of thousands from seed and offsets; and seem to be even more valuable for outdoor growth than for the conservatory or garden frame.

And all we have now spoken of, and much more, may be accomplished with but little skill, if taste exist, and reasonable attention be paid to aspect, air, light, water and cleanliness, and to watching against snails, slugs and such-like visitors; and in some places against cats, dire foes to town-gardening.

But, notwithstanding every difficulty, even tyros are surprised, after some perseverance, at the amount of comparatively inexpensive pleasure they enjoy, partly in giving pleasure to others.

We may well expect that the judicious care which Sir Arthur and Lady Olive Guinness will bestow on the alterations they are commencing in St. Stephen's-green will make it, as to ornamental plants, the most interesting city square in the kingdom; and that whatever head devises the improvements will bear in mind that the placing a shrub or other plant a few feet from others one way instead of another may give it opportunity of being ornamental or unsightly.

ROCK GARDENING.

The increasing attention which this subject has of late received may lead us to expect corresponding improvement in various ways; and everywhere there is room for indulging taste in design, and proving skill in execution. Let us have but a few feet of ground to spare in a city area, or acres of inland glen, or of wild and picturesque sea-side slope, we may find a gem to suit each nook and cranny; and many lovely plants look better in such places than on level ground. It is found not easy to prescribe specific rules as to the construction of all rock-gardens, so much depends on situation and general circumstances; but I venture on a few suggestions which may be generally useful. Good drainage and material in the foundation and lower parts, and provision for escape of superfluous water are important. Room is to be allowed for roots of the plants; and as a general rule, straight lines should be avoided, and straggling and coarse-growing plants. Further, I will here only refer to a few authorities, which I have found interesting to myself, and name a few plants and rock-gardens which are likewise so. At page 270 of *The Garden* for 1877, is an alphabetical list of some few hundred Alpine plants for ornament in rockeries, some of which are, with a few others, here mentioned:—

Acantholimum,
Achillea clavennæ,
Adonis,
Æthionema saxatile,
Ajuga Genevensis,
Alyssum,
Andromeda tetragona,
Anemones,
Astragalus,
Bulbocodium vernum,
Campanulas,
Cordylines,
Cyclamens,
Cypripedium spectabile,
Daphnes,
Dianthus,
Draba violacea,
Echeverias,
Ericas (Heaths),
Erythrinas,
Funkias,
Gazania splendens,
Gentians,
Gladiolus,
Hyacinths,
Iberis,
Irisses,
Lythospormum prostratum,
Narcissus,
Penstemons,
Primroses,
Ranunculi,
Salvias. The lovely blue *S. patens* has stood out for years in an open border, with turf-mould or cinder thrown over the roots for winter.
Saxifrages, in great variety.
Scillas,
Sedums,
Sempervivum,
Symphitum pictum,
Statices, and other sea-coast plants.
Trollius Asiaticus,
Veronicas, in great variety.
Violas,
Yuccas,
Zauscherneria Californica.

Nertera depressa, from Southern America, is a dwarf creeping herbaceous gem when profusely covered with its bright little orange berry. I have seen it at Bitton, amongst Mr. Ellacomb's hardy ferns, whose fronds shelter and partially shade it, and elsewhere flourishing out of doors; and now plants can be purchased for a few pence.

Eritrichum nanum, which inhabits many European mountains, is amongst the brightest of Alpine gems. It is said that its intense blue is approached only by that of dwarf Gentians, whilst its azure hue is like to that of a deep-blue sky, seen from its native hills. It is found from the south of France to Carniola, in stony places, fed by snow rills, at elevations of from twelve thousand feet downwards.

Just now Begonias—named from the botanist Begon, and of which several species have for a considerable time been favourites—attract particular attention, and are very valuable in different kinds of town-gardening. Already many brilliant varieties from Peruvian Andes, of the group to which the *B. Veitchii*, *B. rosæflor*. *B. Clarkei*, &c., belong, though not known more than a few years in England, are amongst the brightest ornaments in summer of many rock-gardens, and at other seasons also of the conservatory. The first of those above-named withstood in Mr. Veitche's garden a temperature of 25° Fahrenheit, which, considering the elevated region where it is native, led Sir Joseph D. Hooker to expect, or at least hope, that it would stand outside at Kew. But as yet none of the family has there borne the combined effects of a winter and spring's cold and damp, though they bloom on a rockery beautifully during summer, and are easily afterwards preserved.

B. Davisii, recently found near Chupe, in Peru, at an elevation of 10,000 feet, is thought by many to excel all other known tuberous-rooted varieties, from brilliance of colour and compactness of habit. It is figured in the *Botanic Magazine* for 1876, Tab. 6252.

I have learned from a faithworthy and experienced gardener, that some pieces of roots of the same group as *B. rex*, which happened to be in soil which he took from within a house to enrich a holly he was planting outside, in the month of March, grew up in summer, and flowered under the tree's shade, and lived there throughout the next winter and spring. That happened in the Queen's County; and in the month of September I saw in a nook, outside my friend Mr. Jessop's fernery, at Cabinteely, more than one young plant of a like kind, which grew there without having intentionally been planted there.

Heterotropa Asaroides, called also *Asarum Japonicum*, is a peculiar-looking little plant, for which we are indebted to Japan, with leaves mottled somewhat like those of some Cyclamens. Though generally treated as an indoor plant, I believe it will bear our winters in many places. Spring is its blooming season.

Arenebia echioides, with yellow flowers, somewhat resembles in general appearance *Lithospermum fruticosum*, whose bright dark blue makes it a valuable feature on rockeries.

Though the loveliest Clematis, and Lapagerias, rosea and white, may be called straggling, there are many places in rockeries and rock-gardens where they would be beautiful features. And now they are increased by thousands from layers, and eyes, and seed. Sometimes the branch for layering is wholly severed from the parent plant.

The first specimens of this rock-gardening which attracted my attention are the fernery at Glasnevin, and the rockeries in the Edinburgh Botanic Gardens; the latter I had the advantage of seeing on different occasions, in company with Mr. Mac Nab, in its early and more advanced stages.

One of the last of such gardens which presented much of novelty to me is that of Sir Francis Brady, Bart., at Sorrento, near Dalkey; where, amongst several plants ordinarily grown under glass, some little shrubby *Diosmas*, and some of *Erica Mac Nabiana E. Hyemalis*, are now in vigour, after living outside for a few years. Here also *Griselinea macrophylla* is, I hope, proving that in some parts of Ireland this beautiful shrub will flourish in sheltered spots, at all events in a young stage of growth. It stood out well for a few years at Mr. Riall's, Old Conna, county Dublin. I have some hope that it may succeed as a city or town ornament, with more or less of protection in winter season.

At the southerly side of Edinburgh the grounds of Mr. James Cunningham, at Blackford Brae, have been skilfully laid out by Mr. Gorrie, landscape gardener. Taking advantage of the peculiar sloping bank at rere of the dwelling-house, and of lessons which Mr. Mac Nab taught the public at the Botanic Gardens, as to construction of rockeries, Mr. Gorrie has constructed one of considerable extent, studded with various suitable plants. In the People's Garden, at our Phœnix Park, at Glasnevin Gardens, at Powerscourt, at Mr. Jessop's, Cabinteely, near Dublin, in different places in the county of Meath, and in many other parts of Ireland, though still too sparse, there are rockeries and rock-gardens where very interesting experiments are being carried on, some inside and some outside. In many places, sheltered from prevailing winds and peculiar local severity, and sometimes with partial or temporary covering of glass, slate, or otherwise, plants will even flourish which, without such care, would inevitably perish. Throughout the country are countless ravines where homes may be made for lovely varieties of the Fern and Moss groups, natives of New Zealand, of Japan, and other countries, hitherto untried amongst us out of doors, and which, with temporary protection, may luxuriate all the year. In a shady, sheltered corner of the small garden of William

Andrews, Esq., near Monkstown, Dublin, are many such plants, from seed which he brought from New Zealand, and some of which I have not seen in so good condition elsewhere.

TREES AS STREET ORNAMENTS.

Patriots little foresaw the improvements which Dublin has already made, when predicting the results of our Legislative Union :—

> "How justly alarmed is each Dublin cit,
>   That he'll soon be transformed to a clown, sir!
> By a magical move of that conjuror, Pitt,
>   The country is coming to town, sir!
> Thro' Capel-street soon, as you rurally range,
>   You'll scarce recognize it the same street;
> Choice turnips shall grow in your Royal Exchange,
>   Fine cabbages down along Dame-street.
> Wild oats in the College won't want to be tilled,
>   And hemp in the Four-Courts may thrive, sir;
> Your markets again shall with muttons be filled—
>   By St. Patrick, they'll graze there alive, sir!"

The arboriculturist Mr. A. Mongredien, in his *Heatherside Manual*, and elsewhere, states that the Levant Plane (*Platanus Orientalis*, or *digitata*) is hardier than the Western *P. occidentalis*, from America—disregarding smoke, soot, and malaria of our cities, as it is seen adorning parks, and squares, and grounds about the Law Courts and churches of London. That some such trees, be they *Planes*, *Elms*, *Ash*, *Ailanthus*, *Acacia*, *Maples*, *Paulownias*, or others as yet unproved, would thrive even in our Sackville-street, and in other streets and roads may reasonably be expected; that all would succeed without need of frequent replacement, any more than in Paris, can scarcely be even hoped. Healthy trees should be selected—not what may be called poles. In some localities, and in some circumstances, varieties of *Ilex*, of *Evergreen Oaks*, of *Aucubas*, and of other evergreens of the *Pine* groups, where smoke does not interfere, &c., may be very appropriate along sides of streets; but judgment is much needed in selection of plants. I have seen *Privets* called evergreen, *Ligustrum ovatum*, &c., grafted on long stems, growing as single trees round courts of the noblest palatial residences in Italy.

PLANTING ABOUT RAILWAY STATIONS, ETC.

Already railway banks, and other patches of ground adjacent to stations in various places, and varying in extent, are planted so as to be features of considerable interest. The first which I particularly noticed is that at Falkirk; afterwards the noble group of Douglas' lordly Pine at Dunkeld; and since, the little garden, thirty feet long by seventeen, at rere of the Salt-hill station, near Dublin, Mr. Kelly, the station-master, has transformed into a gem, for which, justly, he has been presented with a medal by the Royal Horticultural Society of Ireland, and been honoured by visits from the first personages in the country. At some railway stations in England and in Italy, and elsewhere, I have observed promising advance in ornamental planting. Many such places may contribute to the revenue of Companies and nursery gardeners, by arrangement for exhibition and sale of plants and flowers, somewhat in analogy to what is everywhere seen for sale of books and periodicals.

There are very many such places throughout the country, where Camellias and Magnolias would flourish on walls, or even as standard bushes in sheltered nooks, or surrounded by shrubs, and present quite beautiful pictures in early spring, alone or with Rhododendrons, &c. Lately, a bush of *Camellia* was killed at Stedalt, near Balbriggan, by moving it after growing there for fifty years. Nearly twenty years ago, I saw above one hundred flowers on it at one time in March; and one winter or spring after that, it had above one thousand blooms. It was of the semi-double, cherry-coloured kind, called *Doncklacrii*. It is not generally known that amongst modes of propagating this lovely shrub is by cuttings in bottles of water, as myrtles and other plants are sometimes rooted. They rather like high, exposed situations; but in shelter, and not requiring peat, they dislike limestone soil.

GROUNDS ABOUT CHURCHES, ETC.

Grounds about some churches and graveyards, where intramural burial has ceased, have been neatly planted ; and even cemeteries, by judicious planting, are made to contribute to a serious cheerfulness, not unbecoming to persons visiting places of Christian sepulture. As I visit such scenes, I think we do injustice to the spirit and genius of Christianity by planting about mere mortal remains of departed spirits only such trees as Napoleon's willow, or gloomy kinds of cypress :—

> " Dark tree, still sad when others' grief has fled,
> The only constant mourner o'er the dead ; "

or even the handsome *Huon Pine* (*Dacrydium Franklinii*). The devoted women who followed their adored Master to Calvary and the tomb, on returning to that first place of Christian burial, to weep over Him whom they little expected to see so soon again, received the glad tidings which have sustained, encouraged, and even cheered in all trials nearly nineteen centuries of His followers.

BOTANIC GARDENS.

A standard cyclopædia describes Botanic Gardens as establishments wherein plants from all climates and all parts of the world are cultivated, to impart information and improve science, partly for pleasure, partly for luxury. To Theophrastus, who wrote a history of plants, is often ascribed the honour of establishing the first public Botanic Garden, which he bequeathed to his pupils. A disciple of Plato and of Aristotle, he is said to have had the profundity of the latter, with the fascinating eloquence of Plato; and Aristotle named him Theophrastus, or the Divine teacher.

We read that Attalus Philometor, king of Pergamus, and Mithridates Eupator, of Pontus, vied with each other in establishing gardens for cultivation of poisonous plants and their antidotes; and biography tells us of one of the most fascinating female sovereigns of antiquity being not a little practised in such arts. When Antony was in Egypt, abandoning himself to the guidance of Cleopatra, he feared and distrusted her, and insisted on her tasting viands which she had presented to him. On one occasion, deriding the futility of his precaution, she placed a chaplet on his head, and in the course of the banquet invited him to throw the flowers into his goblet, and quaff them with the wine. When about to pledge her, she abruptly stopped him, and commanded a condemned criminal to swallow the draught. The flowers had been steeped in poison; the wretch fell dead at her feet.

The language of Pliny the elder, in his elaborate work on Natural History of Plants, written at the commencement of this era, is so applicable to our day, that I venture to quote a few lines. He asks "Who does not readily admit, that now, when intercommunications have been opened between all parts of the world, thanks to the majestic sway of Rome, civilization and the arts of life have made rapid progress, owing to the interchange of commodities, and the common enjoyment by all of the blessings of peace; whilst at the same time a multitude of objects which formerly lay concealed are now revealed for our indiscriminate use?" In our day, in the management of Botanic Gardens, are men who regularly correspond with other learned men at the head of great gardens elsewhere. The gardens made by Matthæus Sylvaticus, at Solerno, in the fourteenth century, were, perhaps, more of the modern Botanic Garden than any which had before been known. About the year 1333, the republic of Venice established a public medical garden, and had paintings made, some of which still exist, of many of its plants. I found there a good collection of soft-wooded as well as other plants, and I purchased a few of the rarer Yuccas, &c., at reasonable prices. Naples, Turin, Bologna, Ferrara, Padua, Pisa, Pavia, Florence, Rome, and in France, Montpellier, and other cities followed the example of Venice; and all of them, many of which I have seen, are full of interest to the inquiring and observant visitor. We need not discuss special distinctions between what are called Botanic and other gardens. This, however, seems plain, that in the present circumstances of horticulture, such places are specially favoured with opportunities of giving pleasure and information to multitudes, and of advancing civilization in most agreeable ways. One of many important functions, which daily develops itself, is naturalizing plants of foreign countries. The Report for the year 1875 of the Director of Kew Gardens gives some idea of the extent to which interchange of plants and seeds takes place between Botanic Gardens of this country and Gardens of the continent of Europe, and of Asia, Africa, America, Australia, and New Zealand.

Volumes might be devoted to even sketch what is a-doing in Botanic Gardens with which I am myself acquainted; but there are many particular plants which are now so interesting, for trial out of doors, that I may mention a few of them here. And cheapness of glass, and large introduction of foreign plants, enable thousands of persons to try experiments which heretofore were confined to such gardens as we here speak of, and a few wealthy individuals. Palms, and a few kindred groups, are amongst the first plants to which I invite attention, both from peculiarity of their foliage, and from the little that has yet been done in growing any of the few hardy kinds as permanent ornaments out of doors amongst us. When Pliny wrote about introduction of a few kinds into Italy, it was thought that only in tropical climates would any of them mature fruit; but in the collection of my friend Mr. Edward Cecil Guinness are strong young plants grown from seed which I saw gathered, and was given in the Orto Botanico at Rome, within but little distance from the Vatican, in September, 1872, and some of which graced a drawing-room of Mrs. Guinness for several weeks last spring. The fruit was so immature when gathered, that I feared it would not vegetate; however, I myself have one of the plants, which I cherish with classic interest; and what amateur would not do so in like circumstances? Whip me the Stoic!

Many of these plants produce fruit out of doors in our Islands, and one has done so more than once at Glasnevin, but I have not seen any ripen. This Chinese species has borne several severe winters in a cold district close to York, and in the county of Donegal, and elsewhere in Ireland. Above ten years ago, Mr. Backhouse planted in his nursery garden, near York city, two young specimens of this Chusan Palm, which experienced visitors in a few years afterwards expected to see succumb to the first severe spring; but they have continued to advance and grow to vigorous bushes, nine feet high and upwards; and I believe others of the same kind have been planted there with good hopes of success. Nearly forty years the dwarf European Chamærops has held its place in a green sward facing the old range of glass at Edinburgh Botanic Gardens; and a few years ago, Mr. MacNab told me that he attributes an improved appearance, which I noticed, to his having left it unmatted the few previous winters. On the same occasion a specimen of *Fortune's Palm*, or of *C. ex-*

celsa, had recently been moved from a conservatory to the same sward; and though it seemed likely to lose much of the foliage formed in the warmer place, he expected it to retain what would grow outside; and so I believe it has done. Recently young plants and seed of a very ornamental Palm have been introduced amongst us from near the coast of North Western America; and it is hoped, and by many expected, that they will prove as hardy as the Chinese Chamærops, or South American Areca. *Brahea filamentosa* is one of the names by which it is known, also *Pritchardia filifera*, and I believe *P. pacifica*. It is figured in *The Garden*, May, 1876.

In autumn of the year 1870, Dr. Moore, of Glasnevin, encouraged by the progress he had lately before seen made by the plants at York, moved from a conservatory to a sheltered place at rere of his dwelling-house the strong specimen of *Chamærops Fortunei*, then some seven feet high, mentioned above, and one about three feet high, of the South American Palm *Jubæa spectabilis*. Early in the following autumn, he likewise transferred to a bank near Addison's Walk a goodly plant of *C. Khasiana*; and since that he planted in a recess in front of the metal range another variety of *Chamærops*. Some experienced men consider early autumn the best season for such transplanting after the spring and summer's growth indoors. Striking contrast between the foliage of these two latter shrubs and some which are considerably lacerated by storms, in exposed situations, warn against expecting any of the family to withstand all vicissitudes of our weather and climates, wholly unprotected and unscathed.

Perhaps enterprising men in trade, or amateurs, may import from their native countries strong plants of some of the Palms which have a reasonable hope of looking well out of doors in Ireland; and with this view I also name *Areca sapida*, from New Zealand, and *A. Baueri*, from other southerly islands. A few years ago, friends procured for me from Spain a few vigorous stumps of that country's native *Chamærops*; but they have not yet made as handsome specimens as younger plants, seedlings, probably would now be.

About the time of first moving Palms at Glasnevin from within to try outdoor life, a *Cordyline* or *Dracænopsis*, which had spent some quarter of a century in the conservatory, under the name *Dracæna Australis*, gave its place to something more requiring indoor protection, and took its stand in an open border near to the entrance gate. Here it for the first time flowered; and it ripened seed, from which there are young plants. Round the stem, which is about nine feet long, is wound hay rope at the approach of winter; and this plant alone would encourage to perseverance in such experiments. But the same, and one or more varieties, have stood out in many parts of Ireland inland and near the sea, and without any special protection; and in both situations they have ripened seed. The stem is straight, and grows many feet high. In Hooker's *Flora of New Zealand*, the country of the Cordylines, he names and describes several species, some of which are almost unknown in Ireland—at all events in outdoor culture.

A few years ago, I particularly observed in a conservatory at **Kew young plants of** *Cordyline Banksii*, the first of the species I knew of in this country. One of these made its way to Glasnevin, and has spent the last few years in an open border, where it has grown into a vigorous tuft; from several shoots of which there were, in July, 1876, strong stems with abundance of flower, which afterwards seeded. The first of the species which I know of having bloomed in Ireland is at Merton, near Queenstown, county of Cork, where I learn it has flowered yearly for the last six or seven years, but without ripening seed.

By far the showiest of this group which I know of having borne an Irish climate is *Cordyline indivisa*, from New Zealand. The only place where I have seen it permanently out of doors is Lakelands, near Cork, where it has been in a garden border several years. There, in 1874, I saw three plants forming a group which appeared to be offsets from one centre plant that decayed or was taken away. The principal leaves of each of those which I saw were about four feet long, and somewhat more than four inches broad in the widest part, of peculiar olive green, with an orange stripe or rib along the centre of each. Some years ago, this very ornamental and interesting plant could be purchased for a few shillings; and now, I believe, from half a guinea to a pound, or more, is asked for a young plant. Thrice I have received seed from its native home, not a grain of which, though in most experienced hands, has vegetated. Seed from some of the first houses in London, described there as of this plant, has grown with me and others, but not one seedling proved to be what it professed to be—for which, however, I do not undertake to censure any-one. In the summer of 1876, a friend, Fletcher Moore, Esq., when moving from the sea-side, near Dublin, to reside inland, gave me a plant of the Cordyline called Charlwoodia, which had stood in his garden near the sea for at least nearly fifteen months, without special protection; and I have it, looking well, in town ever since, out of doors and uncovered. In that same neighbourhood, near Salthill, another species—very different from any I have above named—has borne the last two or more winters or springs, out, in a very sheltered corner of the garden of William Andrews, Esq. I believe this plant, which flowered well there, is more of what is now named Dracæna than any of those others.

Yuccas, which are akin to the last-mentioned families, have established such reputation in this country, particularly for city ornament, that I again refer to them; and because my making a pretty good collection is much owing to watching the progress of those at our own and some foreign Botanic Gardens. Though most species bear Irish climates, and at least one kind was introduced into England so early as the sixteenth century, I believe there were but a few plants in our city till I introduced several from my small garden at Malahide to Merrion-square, about the year 1861. There are now in its borders above a hundred healthy specimens of the kinds most commonly grown. Hitherto all varieties of *Y. aloifolia*, a species known in England since about the year 1700, have been treated to greenhouse care, with rare exceptions. One of these was for many years in a conservatory at Glasnevin, and I have known it outside there for the last fifteen years, during which time it has produced a few suckers, and looks likely soon to flower. It is one of the fleshy-leaved species now common in Italy and other parts of the Continent; and from the place where it is at our Botanic Gardens, it abundantly proves the hardiness of the species in many parts of Ireland.

The variegated varieties, called quadricolor, and others, may be less hardy than the green; but, with glass, or a board, or some cover overhead for winter, I expect to see most kinds grow out permanently in this country.

Amongst the species which for some years attracted my particular attention at Glasnevin, was *Y. Treculeana*, under the name *Y.* or *Agave Canaliculata*, which is one of several synonyms by which it was long known. Till the last very few years it was scarce in this country; but, having flowered and fruited in more than one part of France, and from the admiration it attracted amongst the few persons who saw it, seed and seedlings have been introduced freely enough to make it now pretty well known amongst us. In a small but interesting nursery-garden, at Place Beau-Sejour, in a suburb of Marseilles, I found a good collection of Yuccas, and at reasonable prices. I saw a plant of *Y. Treculeana* standing six feet high, which the proprietor, Mr. François Ferrand, had shortly before my visit in autumn, 1873, sold for three hundred francs. I bought some seedlings of this variety, and in the nursery of Mr. Durand, at Bourg la Reine, near Paris, I bought, amongst others, a pretty strong plant of the same. This plant, with little suffering, from which it soon recovered, bore the severe winter of 1871-2, when the thermometer fell below 25° centegrade, which was much lower than its average coldest point near Paris. This species has also stood out well the last few years at our College Botanic Gardens. At F. Ferrand's I also bought a few young plants of *Y. quadricolor*, of which he was growing several from cuttings made of sprouts from an old decapitated stump, some two and a-half feet or more high. The head, which he cut off in spring, was forming a handsome young plant.

Y. filamentosa variegata has lived out many years in a border at our Trinity College gardens; and though Mr. Bain occasionally covered it in winter, he often told me that he thought it should not be covered in this climate.

Yuccas, Cordylines, and kindred plants grow well in good ordinary sandy loam.

Some *Darlingtonias* have borne uninjured seven or eight degrees of frost near Dublin.

At the commencement of these pages, we found many Ferns, Mosses, and kindred groups—holding important place amongst ornamental plants, and even in the heart of a smoky city. So far as I know, our best Botanic Gardens have still an important privilege, of showing to amateurs, and all who can learn, that there are varieties of these as well as other families, whose aptitude for growing out, covered or uncovered, in many parts of Ireland might be predicated, and of which but little trial has been yet made. It may be one peculiar province of such Gardens to exhibit to the public specimens of lofty Palms, and Tree Ferns, and of many other tall exotics, which will not grow outside in our climates. For such purpose glass buildings are required, of height and dimensions unsuitable for ordinary gardens; and, generally, the same amount of expenditure on a much smaller scale in private places affords much more actual beauty, pleasure and satisfaction. Occasionally, here and there, we find specimens of such plants as I refer to, from tiny Moss to young specimens of giant Tree Ferns, undergoing trial, judicious or otherwise. But what can yet be achieved by skill and care in favourable circumstances perhaps only sometimes appears to a picturesque mind, like glimpses a saint hath of heaven in his dreams.

In the autumn of 1874, I saw two healthy specimens of *Dicksonia Antarctica* in a nook amongst the bamboos, in what is called the Bamboo Island at Fota, in the county of Cork, and I believe they have lived well there since without further protection. For some years the same Tree Fern stood out in the Island of Arran, down the Clyde.

For the last few years, Mr. Andrews, before-named, has grown out of doors near Monkstown, together with varieties of Pittosporum and other New Zealand shrubs, one of its fine large Ferns, which he believes to be one of the Todeas of that country. Conversations with Mr. C. Mudd, since his botanical searches in India, and inquiries which I have made of other men of knowledge and practical experience, satisfy me that I am safe in expecting to see successful trial out of doors in Ireland of many foreign and very ornamental Ferns which as yet have not been out one winter here. Mr. Mudd tells me that he found varieties of *Alsophila* in India, where snow was knee-deep, and sharp frosts betimes, and where he likewise saw a species of the Palm Seaforthia new to him.

At Powerscourt, at Bitton, at Lord Gough's villa near Dublin, and in other places, I have specially noticed isolated specimens of different foreign Ferns from southern regions, and from North America, Japan, and Continental Europe—just enough to show how little has been as yet done, and to encourage perseverance and experiment.

Amongst ornamental exotics which I believe Dr. Moore is the first to grow outside in Ireland, are varieties of that handsome Lily, *Crinum*, from Southern Africa, which have justly attracted attention at Glasnevin for the last few years, and which I have seen there in fresh bloom so late as the close of November.

I cannot omit to mention the extensive group known as Orchids, than which no plants now attract more general admiration in a high order of gardening. Of terrestrial Orchids, which grow on or in the ground, there are some kinds native to Ireland; and I look forward to very interesting results from hybridizing these with hardy foreign kinds—of which there are several of somewhat like character, and much handsomer.

The only *Cypripedium* indigenous in this kingdom is *C. calceolus*, which was last found in Yorkshire some years ago; but there are species native to woods of Russian Asia and Eastern Europe, up almost to the Arctic Circle, and other foreign species which suit our climates, amongst which may be particularly named *C. spectabile*, from cool parts of North America, and which, being easy of culture, and of increase by division of root, may soon be familiar amongst us.

Disa grandiflora, from the Table Mountain of the Cape of Good Hope, is esteemed as the loveliest of terrestrial Orchids; and from the severity it endures in its home, it is hoped that when the way of treating it outside in Ireland is hit upon as well as proper indoor culture is now known, it will winter here out of doors. Trial is being made of wintering it under cap-glass or garden frame, and having it uncovered for summer.

Many epiphital and parasitical Orchids bear, and even thrive and bloom much better under, cooler treatment than they have been wont to receive in this country. Much has been written to demonstrate this; and Mr. John Bain, of our Dublin College Botanic Gardens, with whom I have had frequent opportunity of conversing on the subject, has shown me many instances of the benefit of admitting abundant air to some of the loveliest of those plants, which for years seldom were given any from outside. In August, 1876, Mr. Mudd, already named, showed me, amongst many very interesting plants lately found by him in India, strong specimens of *Cymbidium elegans*, of *Sologni ocratea*, and of another, or others, of the same family which he gathered at an altitude of 9000 feet up the Himalayas. He also showed me a lovely *Saccalabium*, I believe new, of his discovery, suited to a cool house.

What are called epiphital Orchids, which often are parasites on forest trees, particularly in tropical countries, compose one of the largest and loveliest families of plants with which we are acquainted. In grotesque resemblance of many of the flowers of this family to butterflies, and other of the insect tribes, and even to birds and animals, devotees to what is called Darwinism find abundant material for study, comparison, and contrast.

Almost in the words which Mr. Bain has used in suggesting the growing in baskets, or otherwise, on trees here through great portions of the year, some lovely Dendrobiums, and other Orchids, Mr. Mudd made like suggestions. And he showed me some of his collecting, which he doubts not would well bear such treatment, albeit some folk might deem it desecration.

PEOPLE'S PARKS AND GARDENS.

What are popularly called People's Parks and People's Gardens seem daily to acquire increasing importance. One of the first places of the kind we read of, though very different from what we now enjoy, was the gift above-mentioned by Theophrastus, of his garden at Athens to his pupils. Modern improvements of the parks of London and Paris, and many others, show plainly that statesmen and leaders of the public mind now consider such places for public enjoyment and recreation very important in the present state of society. Some of these, such as Parc Monceau at Paris, from its moderate size and plantings of shrubs and flowers, may appear to be more of gardens than of parcs; but most public parks now have some portion specially devoted to culture of the smaller kinds of ornamental shrubs and flowering plants, which places may well be called People's Gardens. Of this we have a promising specimen in our Phœnix Park, near the principal entrance from Dublin, which may be very pleasingly instructive to vast numbers of visitors who cannot conveniently go often to Botanic Gardens, properly so called. This is one of the first public gardens in this country in which I noticed pretty large groups of some particular plants well grown permanently on rockery. I may again name *Cordylines*, which form a remarkable feature in a well-chosen place. *Aralia Sieboldtii*, sometimes called *Fatsia Japonica;* *Skimmeas, Fortune's Chusan Palm,* and other interesting shrubs are on trial here, and I hope their success will encourage the managers to add to their number, following even at a distance what is adoing in the parks of London and elsewhere.

In admiring or looking at particular plants, with a view to planting the like elsewhere, we should ascertain how far the soil and general circumstances of the different situations correspond with each other, or suit the plants.

For instance, in the Phœnix Park People's Garden, there is a good-sized bed of Rhododendrons, and seemingly in a healthy condition; but the general soil of the country about does not suit this family; and it might be more useful to expend in plants naturally adapted to the soil of the locality the extra money which it takes to import soil for Rhododendrons.

It may be important for authorities to consider how much each hundred pounds judiciously expended in such places would save the Imperial treasury in support of military and police within the next quarter of a century. Perhaps our taste is not sufficiently matured to appreciate such ornaments as make Battersea Park peculiarly attractive; but I venture to suggest that some of the like would be a very useful as well as interesting addition to our People's Gardens. I name a few which are particularly admired in Battersea.

Some Palms, of which I believe *Areca sapida* is one; and *Jubæa spectabilis* may be there, but I did not see it.

Bamboos of different kinds.

Varieties of *Agave*, and others of what are commonly called soft-wooded plants.

Garrya macrophylla, of a small family allied to Aucuba.

Erythrinas, commonly called Coral Trees, in good bloom.

Begonias, named in compliment to the Botanist Begon.

Beaucarneas, Bonaparteas, Dasylerions, Cycads, Musas, Fourcroyas, Aloes; varieties of Tree and other foreign Ferns; and no plant more surprised me than *Pandanus Veitchii* and *P. utilis*, of which I saw several which heretofore have seldom been trusted outside of a warm house, even with such occasional protection as they receive at Battersea.

VILLAS, DEMESNES.

What villas are, as distinct from what are commonly called demesnes, might puzzle us accurately to define; but near to most of our great cities and towns there are houses and grounds which are generally recognised as villas. The Romans, in their most cultivated times, had three kinds—the Urbana, Rustica, and the Fructuaria; but three times three would not count the varieties of our villas, besides those of other countries on the Continent of Europe and elsewhere. We could name hundreds of such near Dublin, London, Edinburgh, and other towns, each with something of special interest; and though there be much variety amongst them, each would be considered deficient without a conservatory and garden, and more or less dress-ground, with ornamental exotics of some kind; and nowhere does the advancing taste of the middle and lower ranks of the community in such matters seem more apparent than in these suburban residences. Though exotic shrubs at Villa Carlotta, on Lake Como, and the collections at the islands in Lake Maggiore, and at Villa Ada on its northern shore, and some in other parts of Italy, are very interesting, the move in this kind of ornamental planting seems as yet but partial in that country of classic villas. Still the most popular guide-books to Italy and to other parts of the Continent seem not to consider their villa grounds as worthy of particular observation. The principal interest which their villas inspire is in their pictures and statues; as to the most celebrated of which an eminent writer, quoted in one of these books, says: "A few Cardinals created all the great villas of Rome. Their riches, their taste, their learning, their leisure, their frugality, all conspired in this single object. While the eminent founder was squandering thousands on a statue, he would allow but one crown for his dinner. He had no children, no stud, no dogs to keep. He built for his own pleasure, or for the admiration of others; but he embellished his country, he promoted the resort of rich foreigners, and he afforded them a high intellectual treat for a few pauls which never entered his own pocket." Doubtless every person with love of the Fine Arts enjoys as a great treat a visit to some of these galleries; but to anyone with a taste for horticulture it is refreshing to go from the dazzling beauty which they present, sometimes with somewhat of sameness, into such grounds as those of Isola Bella, or others about Italian waters, and see the progress ornamental gardening is making there. In 1872 I spent some days at Hotel Tramontano, which was Tasso's Villa, at Sorrento; and two of the proprietors, ladies from our county of Wicklow, seemed quite anxious to introduce into their grounds, where lemons, oranges, and other fruits luxuriate, such ornamental shrubs and plants as would add to the beauty of one of the loveliest spots in Europe. And in visiting these and other show places abroad, and admiring their most ornamental plants, I see very many of the handsomest, whose full beauties Irish climates are particularly fit to develop—for what other in Europe better suits the loveliest evergreens?

At Villa Carlotta, on Lake Como, a specimen of the fine Holly called *Ilex latifolia* (whose leaves are from eight to a dozen inches long), about eight feet high and in full berry, particularly attracted my attention, as the first I had seen in fruit, and by far the healthiest in general appearance. Soon after I saw a somewhat similar shrub in the Orto Botanico at Naples. About two years later, in autumn, 1874, amongst luxuriant shrubs, at Lakelands, near Cork, was one of these shrubs, or small trees, about fifteen feet high, with clean and well-shaped branches, and abundance of ripening berry; and in the following year the same Holly fruited well at Phineas Riall's, Esq., Old Conna, not far from Dublin; and I measured another fine plant there, about fifteen or more feet high.

Though much valuable information be attainable by even an occasional Continental visit, we must now return home to avail ourselves in practice of what we have learned abroad. And here varieties of situation, of climates, and of soils, of villas and demesnes, and of taste and circumstances of their owners, afford opportunities for experiment, and for improving particular families and groups of plants, in ways and to an extent not ordinarily within the province of public Botanic Gardens.

Within a very few miles of Dublin, the dress-ground at Lord Gough's villa, St. Helen's, fairly illustrates what can be accomplished by skill, with a desire to always have a show in the open ground, even in the most trying seasons and in circumstances untoward as to winds and otherwise. The grounds are exposed to modifications of easterly winds, blowing directly in from Dublin Bay, not far distant. Yet, undaunted by difficulties which would deter the inexperienced, and whilst providing for summer and autumn in a style worthy of admiration, the visitor is presented in the months of winter and spring with a very interesting exhibition of hardy herbaceous plants; Dodocatheons, called American Cowslip, of which there are several kinds, I remarked here: and if the handsome, hardy *Cypripediums*, *C. spectabile*, &c., be not already in the collection, I doubt not they will be added if this page come under the eye of his lordship, or any other authority in the place.

Perhaps these grounds are more of demesne than villa; and still more so are the neighbouring-grounds of Lord Pembroke, at Mount Merrion, where a very interesting collection is shown by a skilled and obliging gardener.

I may name, amongst villas near Dublin with which I am acquainted, that of Sir Arthur Guinness on the north, and that of his brother Edward Cecil on the west side.

And amongst Ferneries, those of Mr. Jessop, at Cabinteely; Dr. Hudson, at Merrion; Mr. Westby, at Roebuck Castle; Mr. Stawell Webb, at Monkstown, near Dublin; Mr. Riall, near Bray, may be specially named.

From time to time, and unexpectedly, we see an exotic plant growing out in parts of Ireland, and even well, where we would little predicate that it would survive one winter and spring. Above twenty years ago, on visiting Downpatrick Gaol, during the Spring Assizes, the Governor showed me a rather strong plant of the common Heliotrope, on the garden wall, where it lived from the previous spring; and one of the same kind has been for more than twelve years—how many I cannot say—in an open border of Merrion Square, deciduous late in autumn, and growing up afresh on returning spring. Some years ago, amongst many shrubs in the collection of the late Mr. Whitla, Cave Hill, near Belfast, I was surprised to see one of the Australian Hakeas with ripe nuts—a plant which I had seldom before seen even indoors in Ireland. Afterwards it stood out some years with me at Malahide, and flowered well at close of winter or in early spring.

In more places than one, specimens of the edible tea shrubs are receiving fair trial whether they will more than exist amongst us; I know some in the counties of Wicklow and Cork; and when I had a garden at Malahide I was giving two varieties a trial there, which I had not an opportunity of seeing sufficiently proved.

There are numbers of plants of which it would be

difficult to predicate that they will live out for years in southern counties, and fail in northerly localities, though some parts of Cork, Kerry, and Clare are peculiarly salubrious. But I have been surprised at what I have seen and know in Wexford, Wicklow, and parts of our own county Dublin, and elsewhere, within special influence of mild sea air and shelter.

In some of these places *Ilex Tarago* promises to rival *I. latifolia*; and I have read descriptions of a Holly, from the Sikkim Himalayas, much resembling those two in general appearance, but differing in conformation of the berry, but I have not yet seen a specimen of it in Ireland. Early in the spring of 1874 I observed on one of the specimens of *I. dipyrena*, at Glasnevin, the only berry of this Holly which I have seen ripen in Ireland.

Magnolia grandiflora, Lord Exmouth's variety, is well known throughout Ireland as one of our noblest evergreens. Generally it is grown against a wall; but already in some places it is a handsome standard bush, though I know not one in the country as yet approaching the size which we all have admired in the north of Italy in various places, where betimes there is very trying weather. Varieties have been raised from seed, of which some are finer than others.

A few deciduous species have long proved their hardiness in various districts. *M. tripetala*, *M. Lennéi*, *M. umbrella*, *M. conspicua*, *M. Soulangeana*, *M. glauca*, &c., well deserve careful attention. How far the deliciously fragrant little *M. fuscata* can be treated as a subtropical shrub I cannot say. I have seen it so at Isola Bella, in Lake Maggiore, where winter is often cold and stormy.

At Lakelands, near Cork (Mr. Crawford's), I observed, amongst a choice collection of Rhododendrons in the open ground, *R. Thompsoni* above eight feet high; of *R. Falconeri*, one plant nine feet, and another nearly as high; *R. Dalhousianum*, with abundant flower-bud. A bush of this variety is reported as standing out in Arran, down the Clyde, above ten years, and having one spring one hundred and forty flowers. It was grafted on *R. ponticum*, and never suffered from frost, whilst others of the same kind growing near it were occasionally so injured. Amongst Conifers, I likewise there observed, in the autumn of 1874, *Cryptomeria elegans* and *Araucaria Braziliensis* above twelve feet high and well-shaped; *Dacrydium Franklinii* and *Podocarpus andina*, or *Prumnopitys elegans*—the latter from Chili, whose fruit is edible—about fifty feet high; *Picea bracteata, P. grandis, Abies Devoncana,* and *A. polita. Iseria policarpa,* called also *Polycarpa Maximowii,* is here about ten feet high. This is described as a charming Japanese climbing shrub, with large elegant heart-shaped leaf, and purple berries, which are said to be edible. On different parts of the dwelling-house are vigorous plants of *Berberidopsis corallina,* from eighteen to twenty feet high, which bloom abundantly. *Bignonias,* which I elsewhere mention, are well grown here, and deserve much more general culture in Ireland than they have yet received.

Libocedrus Doniana (*Thuja Doniana*, or *Dacrydium plumosum*, *Kawaha* of the natives), from forests along the banks of the Hokianga river, near the Bay of Islands in the West Island of New Zealand, has for several years stood out well in favourable situations in Ireland. Of many border plants at Lakelands, I much admired the only specimens of the true *Cordyline indivisa* which I have seen winter out in Ireland. The group of three vigorous plants, which were several years out, appeared to be offshoots from one parent, which died.

In outlets of towns and cities, and perhaps within some of them, the evergreen Californian Chestnut, *Castanea chrysophilla*, deserves a choice place. It grows in its native home to a height of forty feet. I have had near Dublin a young pot plant, about two feet high, bearing four nuts one season. In September, 1856, the late Sir William Hooker, when showing me his specimen at Kew, said that he knew but one other in England, both of which came from seed which a collector sent from California. The same evening I wrote to Mr. Frazer, Comely Bank, Edinburgh, suggesting to him to lay a plant which he and I had been for some years watching in his nursery, not knowing what it was. He did so, and at Powerscourt, and Old Conna, and elsewhere in Ireland, are now some of the produce, which promise well.

Oreodaphne Californica has been spoken of as a splendid addition to our gardens, if it stand our winters, which in many places it has done for several years. It is one of the handsome trees for which we are indebted to California, and which at any stage is well worth attention. David Douglass speaks of taking shelter under a well-grown tree which was so sweet, aromatic, and pungent, that it produced such violent sneezing, that even in a hurricane he felt obliged to move elsewhere. A specimen has grown for many years against a wall in the inclosed ground at Glasnevin, always looking healthy; and a large bush is against Mr. Ellacomb's dwelling-house at Bitton. Native hunters make a decoction from the leaves.

At East Ferry, near Queenstown, county of Cork, are interesting collections, which daily become more so, in what may be called villa-grounds, of Mr. Bagwell, Mr. Gumbleton, and others. In the first of these places, I particularly observed *Brugmansia sanguinea* in strong force after surviving some winters out. Likewise at Bitton, near Clifton, where it has lived many years. Lately I observed in the villa-garden of Mr. M'Master, at Simmonscourt, near Dublin, several vigorous shoots, of last summer's growth, from a tuft which has been some years in an open border. These plants have been treated as herbaceous, dying down for winter and spring, and the roots are covered with turf-mould or cinders. I have read a description of a large shrub living out in this country many years, having its stem and branches matted on approach of winter; and if the semi-double kind, called *B. Knighti*, will flourish under such treatment, it may be a beautiful feature in summer and autumn. Ordinary good garden soil suits all well.

Amongst many novelties which I observed at Mr. Gumbleton's is *Fremontia Californica*, which doubtless will soon be well known for its pretty yellow flowers, expanding in April and later. It was discovered by Colonel Fremont a few years ago in the northerly part of Sierra Nevada. It is of the Malva family, and the flowers are pretty abundant at the ends of short spur-like branches.

Varieties of variegated *Phormium*, New Zealand Flax, here proved that they well bear some of our climates, and they are now planted out in many places near Dublin and elsewhere.

I may suggest that in the grounds of many villas there are streams and streamlets, lakes and ponds, whose spongy margins invite experiment with aquatic and many other families hitherto too little grown in such places. In how few of them in Ireland have the *Richardia*, commonly called the Egyptian Arum, and others of the same family, been tried? It is only of late years that *Disa grandiflora*, one of the loveliest of terrestrial Orchids—and which is now imported pretty freely from its native Table Mountain in Southern Africa—was seen amongst us even indoors. Such hardship as it endures in its wild home, and has occasionally experienced in the conservatory in an Irish winter, would seem to imperil its existence; but, like many of the Lily group, it revives, as it were invigorated by what it has endured, and in hands that know how to cultivate it increases manifold from year to year.

Several of the Narcissi, *Narcissus conspicuus*, a richly golden-flowered form of *N. bulbocodium*, or the hooped-petticoat Narcissus, *N. triangularis*, and others, would do well in many such marginal places as I refer to. Tufts of different Primroses—amongst which I would particularly notice new varieties from Japan, for their rich foliage, irrespective of peculiar and ornamental spikes of crimsoned flowers—are well suited for growing on the moist margins of sheltered streamlets.

In like favourable situations, the fresh spring foliage and graceful rosy wreaths of *Diclytra spectabilis* may take their place in company with our choicest flowers.

In a garden of limited extent, at Hammersmith, near London, and in a district whose smoky atmosphere does not specially favour ornamental plants, Mr. Peacock has a most interesting collection of what are called soft-wooded plants, with others: and I believe he and his experienced gardener, Mr. Croucher, manage to make good use of vast numbers of surplus plants, by disposing of them for charitable purposes, and encouraging the growing taste for such pursuits—without encroaching on the province of men in the trade of horticulture.

When I visited Mr. Wilson Saunders' villa at Reigate, in 1872, his grounds, though not extensive, exhibited one of the largest and best collections of outdoor plants, other than forest trees, I have seen. Probably he had the greatest variety of Yuccas in any collection in the kingdom, amongst which were many of the first specimens of their kind introduced into the country, some of which are figured in his *Refugium Botanicum*, and in Curtis's *Botanical Magazine*. Mr. Saunders told me that, after much observation, he inclines to think there are not more than about thirteen distinct specimens known in cultivation.

Outside our great northern capital, on the slopes above the Firth of Forth, and on those looking towards the Pentland Hills on the southern side of the city, several villa-grounds have been recently tastefully laid out and planted.

The collection of Isaac Anderson Henry, Esq., at Hay Lodge, near Trinity, and scarcely a mile northerly beyond the Edinburgh Botanic Gardens, may, like that of Mr. Ellacomb, at Bitton, claim for the grounds, which are of limited extent, the title of experimental gardens. Some very popular favourite plants have been designated *Henrici* or *Andersoni* after Mr. Henry, who has flowered many such plants for the first time in this kingdom, as has likewise happened with other plants at Bitton, under the care of Mr. Ellacomb.

Since the opening of Japan to intercourse with the Western world, under the enlightened rule of its present sovereign, that country has continuously presented us with varieties of ornamental plants new to us, and vieing with each other in beauty and interest. Amongst many whose peculiar loveliness has made them much sought for are varieties of Lilies, of which those called *Lancifolium*, lance-leaved, and *L. auratum*, become everywhere special favourites, and their suitableness for villa gardens, and ease of increase, cannot be too generally known. I have seen a print of one tuft of *L. auratum*, in a large flower-pot, with two hundred and fifty flowers. Generally, I believe, hardy and half-hardy Lilies grow better in the open ground or conservatory border than under pot-culture; and if required in pots, may be moved carefully from the ground, to be replaced when out of bloom. It may not be out of place to tell of a Japanese peasant of whom we have lately read, whose humble grounds attracted the attention of visitors of various classes, and at last were honoured by a visit from the Sovereign Tycoon, who was so pleased with what he saw that he raised the grateful man to the honour of the two-sworded class, as an encouragement to all good gardeners for ever. I may mention a successful experiment by Dr. Moore, at Glasnevin, with some specimens out of doors of *Crinum Moori*, and another variety of the same Cape Lily, *C. amabile*, which have flowered vigorously.

The Pine groups compose a large family of trees, chiefly evergreen, which of late attract much admiration, and of which more may be said when we speak of Demesnes. Comparatively few villas are without some; and too often they are placed as if the planters were ignorant or regardless of the size and height they attain—often within a few feet of windows which they must darken, or be sacrificed when about to develop their character. Many, however, whilst young, are shrub-like beauties, to be judiciously transplanted to grow to forest trees; and, in a younger stage, as pot plants, are very ornamental in rooms. Amongst those may be again mentioned some of the *Cycacidæ*, which are links between Pines and Palms. Of this group, I have known many bear several degrees of frost in conservatories, and experiments are in progress in growing them out of doors. They are ordinary ornaments in Japanese gardens.

We have already spoken of Palms, all kinds of which hitherto in Ireland have been generally kept under glass except during summer-time. There are varieties which from different causes we may reasonably expect to see cultivated in many places altogether out of doors. About the year 1849, the Chusan Palm, *Chamærops Fortunei*, was introduced into Kew, by Mr. Robert Fortune, after whom it is named, and soon proved itself one of the hardiest of the group well called princes of the vegetable kingdom. For nearly quarter of a century a few at least of this Palm have lived out below the latitude of London; but the beauty of some of those which I have seen has been much marred by the effect of winds, though well enduring cold. One such specimen is in the Royal Botanic Gardens, Regent's Park. At Glasnevin, Dr. Moore is trying an experiment for protecting the foliage of one or more specimens. Inserting firmly in the ground around the bush a few posts or poles to the height of or a little above the top of the leaves, he has made of spruce branches rustic screen-work around, but not touching, the foliage.

But by far the finest specimen I know of this group permanently out of doors in the kingdom is one of *C. excelsa,* which was planted by the Hon. and Rev. J. T. Boscawen in his glebe ground at Probus, in Cornwall, in 1853. It is over sixteen feet high, and at six feet from the ground the stem measures more than three feet in circumference. For seven years it has borne many bunches of well-developed fruit. In the same ground is a male plant about ten feet high, growing luxuriantly. We read that this Palm, as well as *Cycas revoluta,* is one of the most ordinary bushes in Japanese gardens, however small the garden may be.

Though the various Italian and other Continental climates differ materially from most of those at home, much valuable information may be obtained for experiment here, by carefully observing what things will grow there, and what protection they require and receive even in and about Naples.

After admiring a fine round bush of *Chamærops Fortuni*, or *excelsa*, some six feet high, on a bank of Lake Como, at Cadenabbia, looking in September as if it never required protection, I was somewhat surprised to learn that it is matted for winter every October.

We see fine specimens of *Dasylerions*, very ornamental, out in Northern Italy; but I believe all these require protection in winter, and I hope to see experiments with some of the group to which these belong, under what is called sub-tropical treatment, in Ireland, and even wintering out with suitable protection. One young *Dasylerion* was planted in a border at Fota a few years ago, near to where I observed a pretty strong *Beaucarnia longifolia*, which I was informed had stood there for some years.

In Battersea Park—whose climate is inferior to those of a thousand localities in Ireland—I observed a few stumps of *Aralia papyrifera*, the rice-paper tree of China, which have stood there for some years, losing their soft foliage on approach of winter, but retaining vitality in the stem to sprout afresh in spring. Other species of ornamental Aralias, particularly *A. Sieboldtii*, have proved themselves valuable additions to villa ornament; so that it is interesting to observe what protection they require in different localities and situations, for in many they will not flourish without some.

From the vigour which *Jubæa spectabilis*, native of far Southern America, has exhibited throughout several years that it has lived wholly uncovered in a sheltered spot at Glasnevin, none need fear to suggest trial of it wherever any Palm will thrive outside. I hope to see the Cabbage Palm, *Areca sapida*, and *A. Baueri*, of New Zealand, and other southern regions, likewise tried amongst us. Cannot strong specimens of these Palms be imported as readily as old Tree Ferns and *Cycacidæ?* and, meantime, young ones may be growing strong and vigorous, and fit for wintering out.

In most of our villas, since the great fall in price of glass which our day has witnessed, are more or less of stove and hot-house, of conservatory and glazed frame; but we try to spare such places for what will not grow as well without protection. There are, however, special reasons for occasionally giving temporary protection to even hardy plants, such as hastening, preserving, or retarding bloom or foliage, for decoration, exhibition, or otherwise. In town gardens, cats too often are dire foes against which we need precaution.

DEMESNES.

Perhaps we might close here with quite enough to afford occupation till continuing advance supplies material for another edition of this little book. I know not a plant in our largest demesne that is not, in some stage, in villa grounds; but the choicest of these are limited in size, and without space for forest trees fully to develop their grandeur and beauty, and compose such features as they do in large demesnes. And now, with admiration of what is already within our reach in the various branches of gardening of which we have spoken, the mind, even of a citizen in the city, seems to enlarge and expand, by prospect of what will yet be accomplished in demesnes of our beautiful island. We may remember how refreshed we saw Socrates, as described by his friend and pupil Plato, by even an evening walk in the outlets of Athens, within whose walls his life was habitually spent. If we continue to advance only at the rate we have gone within our own memory, what a series of gardens will our country present at the close of a century?

Already we have spoken of some country seats as villas, which perhaps might well be called demesnes; but we have increasing numbers of noble demesnes which cannot be mistaken for villas, as to some of which a few words may be added. And though each branch of our subject presents a large field for profitable as well as pleasant employment of women as well as men, and of all ranks and ages, that which we now come to speak of seems to invite the special attention of great numbers of high orders of the female mind, who wish for more suitable occupations than circumstances have hitherto offered to satisfy their aspirations.

In early times of Eastern civilization, Arboriculture was practised by Jews and Greeks, and still more by Romans, for ornament as well as use; and some kind of landscape gardening, on a pretty large scale, engaged the attention of at least a few great women as well as great men.

One of the first instances of which I have heard was designed with artistic skill by the greatest Sovereign of his day, to gratify the taste of a lady. Already we have glanced at those great works which the King of Babylon wrought by captive slaves, to create on artificial hills outside his city ornamental gardens, in imitation of the hills at Ecbătăna, the country of his queen Amytis. We may also remember the reply of King Cyrus the younger, when complimented on the beauty of his hanging gardens at Sardis, that they were wrought by the labour of his own hands. In the polished age of Pericles, at the height of Grecian civilization, Athenian philosophers took much pleasure in such recreations. Cicero and others, in the Augustan age, and many in later days of Imperial Rome, expended large sums in planting and adorning parks for public benefit as well as for their own private enjoyment.

It is interesting to read the description given by the elder Pliny of the introduction into Italy, and attempts to naturalize, Plane-trees, Palms, Euonymus, &c. Amongst his many works, that on Gardening has been saved, so that we may contrast the utmost that had been attained in Augustan days with what is now within reach of ordinary farmers and tradesmen in every civilized country. For centuries from Rome's decline but little advance appears to have been made in Europe, or elsewhere, unless perhaps in China and Japan; but with revival of learning, taste for the subject somewhat revived. Lord Bacon's *Essay on Gardening*—the last edition of which was by Archbishop Whately—is interesting and short. About the close of the sixteenth century, Gerard cultivated eleven hundred kinds of trees and plants; and between that time and 1664, when Evelyn published his *Sylva*, many new species of trees were introduced into gardens and pleasure-grounds in England. We may gather from Arthur Young's *Tour in Ireland* what little advance demesnes here had made a century ago, and how he appreciated the natural aptitudes of the country for landscape gardening. Amongst the few whose ornamental planting he particularly notices are Powerscourt, Collen, Farnham, and Strokestown, which latter has been much improved within a few years by planting new trees suitable to the soil and climate. And in selecting timber trees for ornament or other use, it is specially important to consider soil and climate, and in planting to have regard to prevailing winds. Just now I refer to some observations of Mr. Young, on his visit to Collen, as to the magic power of an improving proprietor, and some of its effects which he saw there; and of late I have myself more than once seen changes greater and on a larger scale wrought at Strokestown, within the last five-and-twenty years, by energy and perseverance of a wise and faithful agent. This country, once a plague-spot of poverty, disease, and degradation, has been transformed into an improved and comfortable district, where attention is now paid to planting for ornament as well as profit. Recently, in looking over some young plantings here, I perceived a few of the Douglas Pine, which happening to be in well-made soil, looked vigorous; and another few, which being in the natural land, appeared far otherwise. Mr. J. Ross Mahon, of whose agency I spoke, and his brother, Sir William Mahon, consulted the experienced nursery gardener, Mr. Madden, at Ballinasloe, as to more extensive planting of this noble tree in parts of Roscommon and Galway, where limestone prevails—little doubting, from the descriptions they read in standard books, that it would grow to a handsome and good timber tree; but Mr. Madden recommended them not to waste money, time, and land in what he doubts not would prove unsuccessful. Magnolias, likewise, he considers not likely to thrive in those places, unless in carefully prepared soil; but I hope they will receive fair trial in different localities.

Speaking of Chief Baron Foster's works at Collen, Mr. Young says: "With no peculiar advantages, but many circumstances against him, amongst which constant attendance at the Courts in Dublin, enabling him to see Collen but by starts, was not the least, the works were left to others at a time when he could have wished to give them constant attention. Twenty-two years before, the whole country was a waste sheep-walk, covered chiefly with heath, dwarf furze, and fern, the cabins miserable, and the whole place yielding a rent of not more than from three to four shillings per acre. His lordship was clearly of opinion that his improvements were very profitable, besides affording him uncommon recreation. His son (the last Speaker of the Irish House of Commons, and afterwards Lord Oriel) took much pleasure in adding to them, and had introduced seventeen hundred sorts of European and American plants." "This great improver," adds our author—" a title more deserving estimation than that of a great general or statesman—has made a barren wilderness smile by cultivation, planted it with people, and made those people happy. Such are the men to whom monarchs should decree honours and nations erect statues. And as to the thieving disposition of the common people, of which he heard much, the Chief Baron, from personal experience, judged them to be remarkably honest; and he said he lived in his house without shutter, bolt, or bar, and, with the place half full of 'spalpeens,' he never lost anything."

Powerscourt, visited or heard of by every tourist, is specially mentioned by Mr. Young. And it is worthy of particular notice, because the Dargle and demesne and the Waterfall grounds appear much more favourably circumstanced for admirers and students of landscape gardening, as they long have been for the artist, than any other place so near Dublin. Here mountain and hill, valley and plain, river, streamlet, and pond, particularly salubrious climate, and all kinds of soils, highly cultivated tastes, and ample opportunities for procuring whatever is most beautiful and suitable, combine in a manner rarely met. Some of the most recent and best works on Forestry speak of the collection of Pines at Powerscourt as amongst the finest in the kingdom.

Some years ago, my namesake of Rathdaire, in the Queen's County, was careful in selecting a choice collection of Pines and of most kinds of other trees and shrubs suitable for that handsome place : and it is deserving of particular notice, as presenting to visitors from the different neighbouring towns—Portarlington and others—a fair field for seeing what will grow in that part of our country.

Several of the demesnes I have been privileged to visit, from Shane's Castle to some in the West and South, supply abundant material for an elaborate treatise on landscape gardening, and ample opportunity for indulgence of refined taste. It is very interesting to see how luxuriantly many of what are considered tender forest trees and shrubs grow in some of these localities. Mr. James Brown, of Stirling, in his work on Forestry, remarks that on the east coast of Ireland, about Donaghadee, the most tender of our forest trees grow with much luxuriance; whilst on the west coast of Scotland, about Portpatrick, but eighteen miles distant, not a forest tree can be coaxed to grow, within considerable distance back from the seashore; to account for which, he dwells on the importance of considering aspect and prevailing winds, which in many places have as much influence as soil.

Here we may name some trees, shrubs, and other plants of different heights, size, and character, which seem worthy of particular attention, and many of which appear not to have as yet received as much as they deserve. Amongst trees of evergreen or persistent foliage, comparatively few Conifers or cone-bearing Pines, or of the berry- or fruit-bearing of the Pine groups, have been long known in this country; but within the present half century many foreign kinds have been introduced, several of which promise to produce valuable timber as well as being ornamental; and volumes, some with beautiful plates, are devoted to their description. *Araucaria imbricata* at Kew, when I was a law student, was the first of the family which particularly attracted my attention, and this Pine has since become one of the most remarkable trees in our plantations. The Araucarians, natives of the Andes, where it is indigenous, are said to be proud of their name, which means frank or free, and they have vast forests of their noble Pine.

It peculiarly enjoys elevated banks, and grows well in dry, airy parks not much exposed to trying winds; and it likes a soil deep and dry and not retentive, where its roots can get down without interruption.

The principal division of Pines seems to be into what are called cone-bearing, and those called berry, or fruit-bearing; and of each I may name a few particularly worthy of attention.

Abies Douglasii, the *Douglas Columbian Fir*, is one of the handsomest, hardiest, and quickest growing introduced into Ireland. It is not half a century since Douglas seemed to have somewhat anticipated his untimely death in a buffalo-pit in the far West, when he wrote about this and other beautiful trees of his discovery, as he says, "lest he should never see his friends, to tell them verbally of these beautiful and immensely large trees." Of rapid growth, and having attained a height of about three hundred feet in Columbian valleys, it has already reached to nearly one hundred in Great Britain. It is not very fastidious as to soil or situation, provided the soil be in a healthy condition, with subsoil cool and porous. I have seen it luxuriate in alluvial vales of Ireland, and in romantic glens and mountain dells of Scotland, and in Wales in *debris* of slate-rocks, and many other places. But in limestone districts I have seen it look unpromising, and I have been advised not to recommend it for these soils.

Timber of mature well-grown trees is fine-grained, elastic, heavy, strong, clean, and easily worked, and capable of receiving a high polish; and there are varieties or forms called *Fastigiata*, *Gregiana*, *Pendulai*, *Taxifolia*, *Variegata*, &c.

P. Cembra, the *Siberian Pine*, is one of the hardiest of our Pines, and not particular as to soil or situation.

Pinus excelsa somewhat resembles *P. strobus*, or the Weymouth Pine, and, deservedly, is in every collection, growing rapidly, but impatient of storm.

P. Hartwegii, *Hartweg's Pine*, is a handsome tree, but I believe does not grow above fifty feet high.

Abies Canadensis, or the *Hemlock Spruce*, is one of the handsomest Firs of American woods, liking deep and somewhat moist soil in sheltered situations.

The Black Spruce, the White Spruce, the Californian Hemlock Spruce, are all pretty well known.

A. Menziesii is very ornamental and hardy, and of rapid growth; and *A. Smithiana*, the Himalayan Spruce, is likewise much admired.

A. Pattoniana, *Patton's Spruce*, grows to great size in the Oregon country, and is said to resemble the Deodar Cedar in habit and general appearance; but it is more thickly branched, and is densely clothed with foliage, and, to some eyes, it is handsomer. This, like other Firs, luxuriates in loamy, porous, cool-bottomed lands.

Abies amabilis, the Lovely Silver Fir, called, I believe, *A. lasiocarpa*, *A. Lowiana*, is a hardy Fir, reaching to two hundred and fifty feet in height, of which a variety is called *magnifica* or *robusta*.

A. grandis, the Grand Silver Fir, one of the noble trees of which Douglas wrote, luxuriates in alluvial valleys, and is quite hardy in many situations.

Of *A. nobilis*, Douglas says he spent weeks in a forest composed of it, and day by day ceased not to admire it; and it is said to be acknowledged by all the Pine race as Picea's Queen.

> " Hail! Nobilis, thy sceptre sway
> O'er Picea's silver train;
> Our homage, Beauty's due, we pay,
> To thy all-verdant reign.

> " Hail! Empress of the Firs and Pines!
> Grand giants! pigmies green!
> What Pine, what Fir its vow declines
> To crown thee Picea's Queen?"

A. Nordmanniana, Nordman's Silver Fir, is a lovely tree, very hardy, and not particular about soil or situation, cold or warm, high or low, and attains a height of nearly one hundred feet.

Perhaps I name as *Abies* some Firs which should be called Pines or *Picea*, and to a learned ear I may make many blunders; but in this, as in subjects connected with my own peculiar profession, I find even great names clashing with names of equal greatness, where both cannot be right.

Pinus Austriaca, Black Austrian Pine, is one of the best known, and for ornament, one of the most useful of the group.

P. Pyrenaica, the Pyrenean Pine, is a majestic tree, hardy and quick-growing.

P. Resinosa, the Resinous or Red Pine, is worth growing for ornament, as well as producing some of the best Pine timber.

P. Pallasiana, or the *Taurian Pine*, is a very handsome kind, but the Austrian Pine is often sold under its name.

P. macrocarpa, or the large-coned Pine, is free-growing, handsome, and hardy, producing cones from twelve to fifteen inches long, and five or six broad, one of which has weighed about four pounds. It is somewhat capricious as to soil, liking good, light, dry loam, deep and porous, and open dry subsoil, and is best where early sun will not fall directly on its foliage.

Bentham's Pine, *P. Benthamiana*, from California, forms a fine tree reaching to two hundred feet in height.

P. Radiata is very handsome as a single tree, attaining a large size and height, and somewhat resembles *P. insignis*, with cones thrice the size of those of *insignis*. The discoverer, Dr. Coulter, with whom I was acquainted for some years, said that its timber is excellent, and much used for boat-building; and I believe it grows well near the sea.

Pinus insignis, justly called the remarkable Pine, is too well known to say more than that it is of rapid growth and tolerably hardy. Rather light, dry, loamy soil suits it, where it has free air without severe winds. Introduced in 1833, it has grown already seventy feet in England.

Of *P. Pinsapo* I have read:—

> " Hail! Pinsapo, thou goodly tree!
> Thou art all grace and symmetry,
> Gem of Iberia's land.
> A pitchy wood tho' we confess,
> Yet perfect lignine these hath less;
> And well thy charms demand
> That thee in rank our strains address
> As next our Queen—our fair Princess."

A few young plants of what is called the Golden Larch, *Pseudolarix Kaemferi*, which was introduced from China into England in 1852, with doubts as to its hardiness, promise so well in the different places I have seen them, that I invite attention to the tree. Deciduous, like common Larch, it attains a height of sixty feet, with leaves double the length and breadth of our own one, and of graceful drooping habit. The largest specimen of this handsome, and I believe valuable, timber tree I know in Ireland is at Old Conna, near Dublin, where it is some twelve feet high, and looks healthy; but some which I saw a few years ago may already have exceeded that height.

Peculiar foliage of some kinds of what are called the Arbor vitæ family invite the planter's attention. The Incense Cedar, *Librocedrus,* or *Thuja doniana,* Don's Arbor vitæ (which, like many other plants, has synonyms), is sufficiently attractive to make it worthy of the care it requires in choice of situation, for it is only in favoured places it stands our climate. Forests along the Hokianga, near the Bay of Islands in the Northern Island of New Zealand, are its native home, where its height is from thirty to about seventy feet. In Ireland I have seen plants in the county of Wicklow and elsewhere looking healthy, but none as yet larger than a small shrub.

L. Dolobrata, the hatchet-leaved, which, a native of Japan, is very handsome, and attains a height of about fifty feet.

L. Chilensis is a beautiful tree from the Chilean Andes, where it reaches a height of seventy feet.

Species or varieties called *Biota,* or the Tree of Life, some of which we see as oval or roundish shrubs, from one to a few feet high, and with golden foliage at certain seasons, are deservedly grown, and are hardy in this country.

Raxopitys Cunninghamii, Cunningham's racem-flowered Pine, from China, somewhat resembling Araucarias, but much less majestic, grows well in some warm shady situations with sweet sandy loam. The best specimen, I know, of what I believe is this Pine, I observed at Shane's Castle.

Some other Cedars are too well known to need description here. *C. Atlantica, C. Deodora, C. Libani, Cryptomeria, C. Japonica, C. viridis,* are favourite trees. *C. elegans* has been justly described as one of the most elegant of recent additions to our Conifers. Lawson's Cypresses, *C. macrocarpa,* and *C. Nutkaensis,* or *Thujopsis borealis, Dacrydium Franklinii,* and several Junipers, *J. drupacea, J. Japonica, J. oblonga pendula,* and *J. Wittmanniana,* are very handsome.

Podocarpus is another pretty distinct variety or kind of Conifer not to be forgotten, but not quite hardy; and *Retinosporas* or *Retinisporas,* some of which attain a height of eighty feet in their homes in Japan, are beautiful, whether as young bushes or well-grown trees. And naming *Salisburia,* or the Maiden-hair Tree, *Saxe-Gotha* and *Sequoias,* one of which is well known as *Wellingtonia gigantea,* and another as *Taxodium sempervirens,* which reaches nearly three hundred feet high in North-West America, enough has been said to give inquirers interesting employment. *Sciadopytis,* or the *Umbrella Pine,* is said to be fastidious, liking loamy, sandy, sweet, healthy, gravelly, porous soil. Sour soil, or very dry situation, does not suit it. It likes a warm, sheltered locality, neither too dry nor too moist, and not exposed or over-sheltered above, also an open, free substratum. It attains a height of one hundred and fifty feet, and the Chinese and Japanese have it dwarfed as well as large, and of variety of foliage.

I now name a few trees and shrubs of other families which attract attention, and some of which perhaps have been already mentioned.

Of Maples, *Acer macrophyllum*.

Negundo fraxinifolium, *N. polymorphum*, from Japan, which latter, probably, is too tender for our climates, unprotected.

Ailantus glandulosa, or the Tree of Heaven, on whose leaves a hardy silk-worm, called *Bombyx Cynthia*, loves to feed.

Ampelopsis, commonly known as five-fingered ivy, of the Vine family, and of which those called *Veitchii* from Japan, are lovely on walls, as is also *A. Japonica* (*Sieboldtii*), from the same country, abounding in beautiful plants.

Amygdalus, or *Almond Tree*.

Andromeda, somewhat akin to heaths.

Aniseed Tree, *Illicium*, stands out in many parts of Ireland.

Aralias, of which also there are some lovely varieties from Japan.

Arbutus Andrachne, *A. procera*, *A. uva-ursi*, a vigorous trailing plant.

Aristolochia sipho.

Aristotelia Macqui.

Azaleas, several of which are hardy.

Berberis Darwinii, &c. Of this group there are very handsome shrubs from Japan called Mahonias.

Buxus, or *Box*, of which I lately procured plants

of a new variety from Japan, which promises well, and is a good town plant.

Calycanthus, or American Allspice.

Camellias, of which hardy kinds form lovely spring flowering bushes or shrubs in North, South, East, and West of Ireland; and I have lately seen a few healthy specimens of Teas, the green and Assam species, which I have known for some years out of doors and uncovered.

Catalpas.

Ceanothus, of which there are evergreen varieties, ornamental on walls, and of rapid growth.

Citrus, Orange and Lemon, of which *Citrus triptera,* or *Limonia trifoliata*, promises to stand out in some of our climates with, and perhaps without, shelter of a wall.

Colletia, belonging to the Buckthorn family, is a very peculiar shrub, and well worthy of a place in collections; and I know not any reason why it may not grow in our towns, and even parts of cities.

Cotoneasters and *Cratægus*, of the Apple family.

Daphne, some of very sweet kinds, are hardy.

Garrya elliptica fœmina fruited several years at Mr. Finzell's, Clevedon, near Bristol. The fruit are about the size of peas, and come thirty or forty together on drooping racemes, some few inches long.

G. macrophylla, or *laurifolia*, has finer foliage, but seems in most localities to require protection of a wall, or other partial protection, in winter.

There are several very handsome Oaks, with evergreen or persistent foliage; and others not so, though some of them retain the leaf fresh much longer than others.

Quercus pannonica, I believe from Siberia, is one of the finest of Oaks, and of rapid growth, producing excellent timber. The Scarlet Oak is also a fine variety, and to be had cheap.

Q. lamellosa, common about Darjiling, is spoken of by Sir Joseph D. Hooker as by far the noblest known species, whether for size of foliage and acorn, or for their texture and colour, or for the imposing appearance of the tree. The wood being indifferent, and the acorns sprouting very soon after ripening, may be reasons for its being but little known in England.

Some Magnolias, from the size they attain in favoured situations, may be classed amongst trees as well as amongst shrubs.

CONCLUDING OBSERVATIONS.

We have sketched our subject so that each of us may select for particular attention any branch that suits our taste. We have seen great men and wise in all times enjoy gardening for pleasure and recreation—when Babylon was in her greatness and Grecian civilization at its height; when King Solomon was in his glory, and Cicero, when one of the busiest leading men of Rome. Lord Bacon wrote an Essay on Gardening, which Archbishop Whately made time to republish, with notes. Napoleon at St. Helena betook himself to such pursuits to beguile weary hours; and the late Emperor expended tens of thousands in ornamentally planting the parks of Paris; which work has already largely encouraged improvement, and creation of such places in the British Islands, and throughout Christendom, and elsewhere. Slight acquaintance with the history of ornamental gardening for the century, up to our day, shows hosts of choice spirits, who attained high positions in various callings, enjoying it as healthful recreation. In the seventeenth century the Dutch mind became almost deranged, from what has been called Tulipomania; when many individuals expended much more than they could afford for a few roots of their favourite flower, and two thousand florins were paid for one of the tulips called Semper Augustus; and ever since, Holland has been a country to supply Europe with various ornamental plants. For centuries—I know not how many—Japan and China have been countries of gardens; and the islands of Great Britain are perhaps more indebted to Japan than to any other country for ornamental plants which suit our climates, and in Japan love of plants and flowers pervades all classes. Mr. Fortune tells us that all the ground about the village of Sumæ-Yah is covered with nursery gardens, and that when he visited that country no other part of the world cultivated so many plants for sale.

Notwithstanding all we read about ornamental gardens, in particular places and at occasional times, within our own memory culture of plants for ornament has made more way generally in the world, and in the British Islands amongst the rest, than at any former period. Pliny the elder, who spent his life in study of natural history, left an encyclopædia of all that was then known of horticulture; but all that was small, and the enjoyment confined to few, compared with what is within reach of millions amongst us. In these later days, from Japan and China to Terra del Fuego and islands far to the south, from North-Western America to Queensland, the world is ransacked to minister to our pleasure in different branches of natural history; and rulers and leaders of the public mind, in countries most distant from each other in many ways, encourage such enjoyments. We all see or hear of what has been done and is a-doing in the parks of Paris and London.

Now, even at risk of seeming to wander from our immediate subject, I will mention a few more of what appear to me special reasons, with a social aspect, for encouraging amongst ourselves such pursuits as those we have been considering. We live in peculiarly intellectual and thoughtful days: never before was the brain so worked: for a century the civilized world has been passing through a social revolution such as it never before witnessed. From time to time, ablest observers and profoundest thinkers have expressed alarming apprehension as to universal increase of what is called democratic power. Little more than forty years ago, about which time De Toqueville visited Ireland, with which he was closely connected, he closes his celebrated work on *Democracy in America*, expressing nervous fears and anxious hopes on this subject of absorbing interest. Even in England we have ourselves seen, within the last few years, our great political champions come down to Parliament fresh from study of Homer and Homeric heroes, and, seemingly impelled by exigencies of party warfare, head their followers in what are called leaps in the dark. Happily, throughout all, a Hand unseen but not unperceived guides advancing civilization; and already the world reaps no little fruit from the efforts made since remote ages to raise the masses from crassest ignorance, slavery, and degradation, and to elevate the more thinking portions to a sense of self-respect and of their proper position in the community.

In this state of society it is all-important to cultivate and encourage whatever tends to refine, elevate, calm, and content; and such recreations as we speak of seem particularly conducive to this end, and suited to the temper and genius of our times. Gladiatorial shows and fights of wild beasts, which fascinated millions and attracted crowds of even high-bred ladies and vestal virgins of Imperial Rome, still unsoftened by Christianity, and with a policy of accustoming her people to scenes of blood, would not now suit the taste of our people or the policy of the leaders of public opinion. In England, up to the time of the Great Rebellion, baiting of animals, and specially of bulls and bears, was a favourite pastime with every class. The last Henry, Queen Mary, Elizabeth, and James the First, encouraged it; but under Elizabeth, growing taste for theatrical representations was giving a new tone to the manners of the rich. When bear-baiting ceased to be their amusement, it speedily declined because of scarcity of beasts; but bull-baiting throughout the eighteenth century continued to be a popular English amusement. In 1729 and 1730, we find advertised amongst London entertainments "A mad bull to be dressed up with fireworks and turned loose in the game-place; a dog to be dressed up with fireworks over him; a bear to be let loose at the same time; and a cat to be tied to the bull's tail; a mad bull, dressed up with fireworks, to be baited." And even Canning and Peel opposed abolition of bull-baiting by legislation. Such amusements were mingled with prize-fighting, boxing matches between women, or combats with quarter-staves or broadswords, &c.

The Drama has held a conspicuous place in the world ever since the days of Susarion in Attica, nearly six hundred years before our era. Horse-races and gambling are to thousands their chief amusements; cricket and golf are national recreations, and other athletic sports take somewhat the place of Grecian and Roman games of ancient times. I well know the fascination of our own field sports, and that they help to manliness of mind as well as vigour of body. The tobacco-pipe and cigar soothe and beguile many a weary hour. Sculpture and painting hold their places in civilized countries.

Napoleon considered encouragement of music of great public importance. One day, at St. Helena, the conversation turned upon the Fine Arts, and one of the company made but little account of music. "You are wrong," said the Emperor; "it is of all the liberal arts the one which has most influence on the passions, and that which the legislator is bound to most encourage. A well-composed piece of music touches and melts the soul, and produces more effect than a treatise of morality, which convinces the reason, leaves us cold and unmoved, and makes no alteration in the slightest of our habits." The old Greek game of cock-fighting was too common in England from the time of the second Henry till recent days. About the beginning of the eighteenth century, one Machrie, a fencing-master, was regarded as a benefactor to Scotland for having started there a new and cheap amusement. In *An Essay on the Innocent and Royal Recreation and Art of Cocking*, he expresses his hope that "in cock-war village may be engaged against village, city against city, kingdom against kingdom—nay, the father against the son, until all the wars of Europe, wherein so much innocent Christian blood has been spilt, be turned into the innocent pastime of cocking." What was called the Welsh main was the most sanguinary form of the sport, where sometimes as many as sixteen cocks were matched against an equal number, and fought till all on one side were killed. Then the victors were divided and fought, and so on till but one champion survived, and we read of the church-bells ringing in honour of the victor.

But of all tastes with which we are endowed, that for natural history in general, and particularly that for Horticulture in its various branches, are perhaps the purest, most elevating, and most universal; and ornamental gardening is said to be the ornamental art which last approaches perfection in advanced communities.

Notwithstanding all we read and hear of the dangers of democracy, communism, scepticism, and infidelity, and of modern science superseding the old religions of the world, never before were the softening and civilizing influences of Christianity so largely apparent in practice as they are in our days. Never were thought and interest on religious subjects diffused over so large an area—though such thought and interest may be too indefinite and confused. The most advanced scientific men of England teach us that "At present there is no book more read than the Bible, no life more deeply studied and discussed than the life of Christ. There is probably a greater amount of earnest attention devoted to these subjects than to any other branch of human inquiry."* Even

* *The Unseen Universe*, Introduction.

controversies, in which religion is inseparably connected with science, are conducted with much less acrimony than characterized them in by-gone times. And never before were half-learned attempts to persuade the masses that we are not creatures of an Intelligent Spirit governing what is called this material universe—and to escape from such superintendence too often very embarrassing even to the best of men—presented to everyone at all literate, in subtle and beguiling forms. Does it not, then, behove all who have the welfare of the community at heart to cultivate whatever tends to prepare us for healthy and cheerful views on such subjects? and these are much influenced by the state of our health and spirits, and these again by our recreations.

History teaches us that, in every stage of civilization, men of largest capacity and highest education have deeply felt the need of the help which Religion alone affords. Such men, with millions of others, may be said to live three lives—the public, the domestic, and the private—much of which latter is unseen and unknown by even the nearest and dearest friends. David Hume said it was a mistake to suppose that he thought in private as he reasoned in his published essays. Cæsar could ridicule in public the popular religions, but he never mounted a chariot without muttering a private charm or secret incantation. Before the battle of Pharsalia he addressed a prayer to the gods whom he denied in the senate, and derided in company of literary friends; and he appealed to divine omens when he was about to pass the Rubicon. Napoleon once was as vehement in professing the religion of Mahomet as Simon Peter was in denying Him in whose service he died a martyr; but some of the most interesting passages in biography describe the fallen Emperor, towards the close of the last of three periods into which his chequered life has been divided, bearing strong testimony to the influence of Christianity on the world at large, and contrasting his own power, when highest, and that of other founders of kingdoms, with what that Religion had already achieved from an origin which appeared most unlikely. Who knows how powerfully the teachings of his infancy, of which he sometimes spoke, were secretly working in a spirit by nature peculiarly intense?

The popular idol, Sir Walter Scott, at a trying time, when he deeply felt the want of human sympathy, and was thinking more of realities than of fiction or romance, found not a little consolation in the belief (which advanced science teaches to be at least quite possible, if not probable) that the spirits of even human friends who have disappeared from this life have, wherever they are, still lively interest in our welfare. On his return to Abbotsford, after a short unavoidable absence, he found the lifeless body of Lady Scott, from whom he had parted but a few days before. He describes himself as lonely, aged, and embarrassed, impoverished, deprived of the sharer of his thoughts and counsels, who could always talk down his sense of the calamitous apprehensions which break the heart that must bear them alone. "I have seen her," he says. "The figure I beheld is, and is not, my Charlotte—my thirty years' companion. Can it be the face that was once so full of lively expression? I will not look on it again. But it is *not* my Charlotte—it is not the bride of my youth, the mother of my children, that will be laid among the ruins of Dryburgh which we have so often visited in gaiety and pastime. No! no! She is sentient and conscious of my emotions somewhere—somehow: *where* we cannot tell; how we cannot tell; yet would I not at this moment renounce the mysterious yet certain hope that I shall see her in a better world for all that this world can give me."

One of the most remarkable sceptical writers of our day and country, Mr. John Stewart Mill, an eminent philosopher, and generally regarded as a sound logician—one for whom a rare plant had a charm—cost what it might of labour and fatigue in its search, the accomplishment was a moment of rapture—in the maturity of his mind, when discussing the bearings of science on religion in general, and its utility, urgently advises all who can to live confiding in that Religion, which he also describes as essentially unlike all others, but for whose enjoyment his peculiar mind seems to have been unfitted by early education. Mr. Mill speaks of "one Man who left on the memory of those who watched His life and conversation such an impression of His moral grandeur, that eighteen subsequent centuries have done homage to Him as the Almighty in person." Again he says: "Religion, since the birth of Christianity, has inculcated the belief that our highest conceptions of combined wisdom and goodness exist in the concrete in a living Being who has His eyes on us, and cares for our good. Through the darkest and most corrupt periods, Christianity has raised this torch on high—has kept this object of veneration and imitation before the eyes of man."

Hear what the historian Lord Macaulay says about the old philosophers:—"God the uncreated, the incomprehensible, the invisible, attracted few worshippers. A philosopher might admire so noble a conception, but the crowd turned away in disgust from words which presented no image to their minds. It was before Deity embodied in a human form, walking among men, partaking of their infirmities, leaning on their bosoms, weeping over their graves, slumbering in the manger, bleeding on the cross, that the prejudices of the Synagogue, and the doubts of the Academy, and the pride of the Portico, and the fasces of the Lictor, and the swords of thirty legions, were humbled in the dust."

But Mr. Mill and other writers, eminent in different branches of science, seem to think it very important that we have not what they consider logical proof of even the fundamental truths of Christianity, leaving everyone in most uncomfortable scepticism and doubt. Though we may not have such demonstration as is vainly sought, and the nature of our Religion declines to reveal, we have intuitive perception on which ultimately all human science depends, and Religion is highest science, beginning where others end. Religious truths are inferences from scientific laws, which are *data* for religious philosophy. One of the deepest and soundest thinkers says, "a little philosophy inclineth man's mind to atheism, but depth in philosophy bringeth men's minds to religion." But its

> "Study is like the heavens' glorious sun,
> That will not be deep-search'd with saucy looks."

The child, the peasant, and the most learned, readily receive its truths; but I believe, in our day especially, the wisest and best of Christian men need no ordinary training: and every help they can anywise receive from recreation, amusements, or otherwise, to cultivate and enjoy such habitual tone and temperament of mind and spirit, that when sorely tried, as tried they are, they can say, "Although the fig-tree shall not blossom, neither shall fruit be in the vines; the labour of the olive shall fail, and the fields shall yield no meat; the flock shall be cut off from the fold, and there shall be no herd in the stalls; yet I will rejoice in the Lord, I will joy in the God of my salvation." But *some* of the most popular amusements we have referred to seem not very conducive to this end.

A few parting words as to the prospects of ornamental gardening in our own island, and aptitude of our people for such enjoyments. England has for a century and a half been spoken of as a country of gardens. About the middle of the last century, the poet Gay wrote that skill in gardening or laying out grounds is the only taste the English can call their own—the only proof of original talent in matters of pleasure. The English garden is proverbial for beauty, and it is said that the English cottage garden stands alone in the world. The gardeners of Scotland are celebrated, partly from the natural difficulties with which they have to contend; but the climates and soils of Ireland are amongst the most favoured in Europe for horticulture in general, and specially for evergreens of various kinds. Centuries ago, Lord Bacon spoke of Ireland as "a country blessed with almost all the dowries of nature—with rivers, havens, woods, quarries, good soil, temperate climate, and a race and generation of men valiant, hard, and active, as it is not easy to find such a confluence of commodities, if the hand of man did join with the hand of nature; but they severed—the harp of Ireland is not strung or attuned to concord."

What Sir William Temple, in his *Essay on the Garden of Epicurus*, says about the climate of England, seems strongly applicable to our island. Speaking of his own oranges and other fruits, he says: "I must needs add one thing more in favour of our climate, which I heard the King say, and I thought new and right, and truly like a King of England that loved and esteemed his own country: it was in reply to some of the company that were reviling our climate, and extolling those of Italy and Spain, or at least of France. He said he thought it was the best climate where he could be abroad in the air with pleasure, or at least without trouble or inconvenience, the most days of the year and the most hours of the day; and this he thought he could be in England more than in any country he knew of in Europe." And here I venture to quote another observation of that eminent statesman and devoted lover of his garden, when he speaks of the temperate habits of Epicurus, and the aspersions falsely cast upon his character by rival sects, and even by some early Christian writers. He says: "I have often wondered how such sharp and violent invectives came to be made so generally against Epicurus by the ages that followed him, whose admirable wit, felicity of expression, excellence of nature, sweetness of conversation, temperance of life, and constancy of death, made him so beloved by his friends, admired by his scholars, and honoured by the Athenians. But this injustice may be fastened chiefly upon the envy and malignity of the Stoics at first, then upon the mistakes of some gross pretenders to his sect (who took pleasure only to be sensual), and afterwards upon the piety of the primitive Christians, who esteemed his principles of natural philosophy more opposite to those of our religion than either the Platonists, the Peripatetics, or Stoics themselves." And now as to the people of Ireland.

Our population is composed of various elements. The eminent writer, Mr. Froude, describes the Celts, who are the primary element of its society, as light-hearted and humourous, with special appreciation of just dealing: "Give an Irishman," says he, "a just master, and he will follow him to the world's end. Possessing a fascination in their own land, and power greater than any other known family of man of assimilating to their own image those who venture amongst them."

And this has been so for many centuries, notwithstanding the most stringent legislation of England against her settlers in Ireland intermarrying with the Irish enemies, and Englishwomen marrying Irishmen. All failed to prevent such unions, at least ever since Strongbow married Eva, with whom he obtained Leinster as a dowry; and the Statute of Kilkenny declared " alliance by marriage, gossipred, amour, or in any other manner, between English and Irish, of the one part or the other, illegal; and that anyone attainted thereof should have judgment of life and member as a traitor." And if the people of Ireland have fascination here, the English have their own wherever they be; and this contributes by intermarriage, and will contribute, more to cement the union of the countries than any legislation can make or undo. But we, Celtic and Anglo-Irish, are conscious of peculiar proneness to listen to beguiling fascination, and to yield to temptation of various kinds; and we need all the help we can obtain, from whatever source, to produce steadiness of purpose and firmness of character; and amusement and recreation have much to do in forming and establishing character. What seem but trivial matters too often mar and spoil lives which otherwise might be happy and beautiful: " Take us the foxes, the little foxes that spoil the vines; for our vines have tender grapes."

In early times this island was far in advance of England in important branches of learning and of fine art. In Dagobert's reign the learned St. Gertrude sent here for masters to teach Greek, poetry, and music to the cloistered virgins of Nivelle. More than two centuries ago Archbishop Ussher ventured to predict that Ireland would become the brightest gem in Christendom. Later, Bishop Berkeley—whose peculiar metaphysical teaching was never more important than in the present phase of mental science and religious thought—asks, amongst his celebrated queries, whether there be any country in Christendom more capable of improvement than ours? The late Dr. Petrie—a learned Irishman and scholar, of Scottish and German extraction, of whom I had the advantage of being for years a pupil in youth, and whose friendship I enjoyed until his death—speaks of Ireland as eminently distinguished in early times for learning, as the cradle of Christianity to the north-western nations of Europe in the sixth and to the ninth century. And Mr. Gladstone, during his recent visit here, when speaking of our Antiquities, of whose existence he said he before knew only in the abstract, expresses surprise at the position which he found she occupied in those remote days: "I may say those centuries when she had almost a monopoly of learning and piety, and when she, nearly alone, held up the torch of civilization—of true Christian civilization—to northern and western Europe." And this is indorsed by our own countryman, Lecky, in his late *History of England*.

However various our opinions may be as to the merits of that great liberal leader, King William the Third, we all may approve of the impulse he gave to ornamental gardening in this kingdom, as we may of Queen Mary's patronage of ornamental porcelain. At the beginning of the last century, probably, there were not more than one thousand species of exotics in England; and we read that in the year 1724 there were only twelve of evergreens, and that five thousand kinds of exotic plants were introduced during the century. Landscape gardening was introduced into Ireland by Dr. Delany, the friend of Swift, whose villa was in Glasnevin; and somewhat about the same period a florists' club was established in Dublin by Huguenot refugees, which, however, meeting but little encouragement, soon expired. The country and our people were not yet ready for such recreations and enjoyments to a large extent or on a large scale.

To have proposed ornamental gardening as a popular recreation in Ireland generally, or even in our city, in days which many of us well remember, when all ranks were suffering from various causes, and hosts of our people were emigrating to seek for homes in strange lands, might have seemed puerile, if not derisive. But, even in those worst of times, many who could look below the surface, albeit they were themselves sorely tried, somewhat confidently hoped to see the country recover, knowing her resources and the elasticity of the national mind, and that whilst

> "The lamentable change is from the best,
> The worst returns to laughter."

She revived, and perhaps sooner than the most sanguine expected; and now all ranks are more or less prepared to appreciate any rational enjoyment; and, amongst many within their reach, that one—not the least—about which I have ventured to offer a few rather discursive hints.

INDEX.

	PAGE.		PAGE.
Abies amabilis,	104	Ailantus glandulosa,	109
Canadensis,	103	Ajuga Genevensis,	52
Devoneana,	84	Almond tree,	109
Douglasii,	102	Aloes,	21
grandis,	104	albo cincta,	22
lasiocarpa,	104	Americana,	21
Lowiana,	104	Alsophilla,	72
magnifica,	104	Alyssum,	52
Menziesii,	103	American Cowslip,	81
nobilis,	104	Ampelopsis hederacea,	30
Nordmanniana,	104	Roylii,	30, 109
Pattoniana,	103	Sieboldtii,	109
Patton's Spruce,	103	tricuspidata,	30
polita,	84	Veitchii,	30, 109
robusta,	104	Amygdalus,	109
Smithiana,	103	Anæctochilus,	15
Acacia Drummondi,	39	Setaceus,	16
Lophantha,	39	Andromeda,	109
Acantholimum,	52	tetragona,	52
Acanthus,	35, 50	Anemones,	52
Acer, *see* Negundo.	109	Aniseed tree,	109
macrophyllum,	109	Anthurium,	40
Achillea clavennæ,	52	Aralia,	76
Adiantum,	13	papyrifera,	93
Adonis,	52	Sieboldtii,	76, 93
Æthionema saxatile,	52	Araucaria,	101
Agapanthus umbellatus,	20	Braziliensis,	84
		Arenebia echioides,	55
Agave, Americana,	21, 35	Aristotelia Macqui,	109

K

	PAGE.		PAGE.
Arbutus.		Box,	109
Andrachne,	109	Bulbocodium vernum,	52
procera,	109	Buxus,	109
Uva-ursa,	109	Japanese,	109
Areca.			
Bauerii,	14, 29, 66, 94	Caladiums,	40
Sapida,	14, 29, 66, 94	Californian chestnut,	85
Arenebia echioides,	55	Calycanthus,	109
Aristolochia sipho,	109	Camellias,	110
Asarum Japonicum,	54	Doncklaerii.	59
Asplenium,	13	Campanulas,	50, 52
Assam tea,	25	Castanea (chestnut).	
Astragalus,	52	chrysophylla,	85
Aucubas,	36	Catalpa,	110
Himalaica,	37	Ceanothus.	
Azalea,	109	dentatus,	28
		intermedius,	28
Balcony gardening,	22	rigidus,	28
Bamboo, Island,	72	Cedrus.	
Beaucarnia longifolia,	93	Atlanticus.	108
Begonias,	35, 53	deodara,	108
Clarkei,	53	Libani,	108
Davisii,	54	Chamædoria Hartwegii,	15
Rosæflor,	53	Chamærops.	
Veitchii,	53	excelsa,	29, 92
Beschorneria Yuccoides,	22	Fortuni,	29, 65, 91, 92
Bignonia.		Griffithiana,	29, 30
grandiflora,	30	humilis,	29, 46
radicans,	30	Khasiana,	65
Beaucarnea,	77	Martiana,	29, 30
longifolia,	93	Charlwoodia,	44, 68
Bentham's Pine,	105	Chusan Palm,	91, 92
Berberidopsis,	26, 84	Citrus.	
corallina,	26, 84	Triptera,	110
Berberis,	109	Clematis,	31
Darwini,	109	Clivea nobilis,	19
Biota,	107	Clyanthus.	
Bonopartea,	77	Dampierii,	29
Brahea, see Pritchardia.		magnificus,	28
filamentosa,	65	puniceus,	28
Pacifica,	65	Cocos.	
Brugmansia.		coronata,	15
Knightii,	87	flexuosa,	15
sanguinea,	86	Colletia,	110

Index.

	PAGE.
Convolvulus,	31
Coral tree,	77
Cordyline.	
Australis,	35, 44, 66
Banksii,	35, 67
indivisa,	35, 67, 85
Corypha.	
Australis,	15
Cotoneaster,	29, 110
Hookerii,	29, 40
microphylla,	29
Simmondsii.	29, 40
Velutinus,	29
Cratægus,	110
Crinum,	73
amabile,	91
Moori,	91
Crotons,	40
Cryptomeria.	
elegans,	40, 84
Japonica,	84
viridis,	108
Cunningham's Racem-flowered Pine,	107
Cycacidæ, Cycas,	15, 77, 91, 92
Cydonia Japonica,	25
Cymbidium elegans,	74
Cypress.	
Lawson's,	108
macrocarpa,	108
Nutkaensis,	108
Cypripedium,	73, 81
calceolus,	73
spectabile,	52, 73, 81
Cyrtomium falcatum,	34
Dacrydium.	
Franklinii,	60, 84
plumosum,	85
Daphnes,	52
Odora,	46
Darlingtonia,	71
Dasylerion,	77, 93

	PAGE.
Davallia,	13
Mooreana or Moorei,	13
Demesnes,	95
Dianthus,	53
Dicksonia.	
Antartica,	27
Dictamnus.	
Fraxinella,	48
Dielytra.	
spectabilis,	88
Disa.	
grandiflora,	73, 87
Dodocatheon,	81
Dons Arbor-vitæ,	107
Douglas Pine,	102
Varieties—	
fastigiata,	103
Gregiana,	103
pendulai,	103
taxifolia,	103
variegata,	103
Draba violacea,	52
Dracœna Australis,	40, 66
Dracœnopsis,	43, 66
Echeverias,	52
Encephalartos M'Kenii,	15
Epacris,	39
Ericas,	55
hyemalis,	55
M'Nabiana,	55
Eritrichum Nanum,	53
Erythrinas,	52
Amasina,	49
crista-galli,	49, 77
herbacea,	50
Escallonea.	
Macrantha,	44
Eugenia.	
Apriculata,	36, 46
Cleken or Clequen,	46
Luma,	46
Ugni,	36, 46
Euonymus,	97

Index.

	PAGE.
Fatsia Japonica,	76
Ferula.	
communis,	49
Persica,	49
tingitana,	49
Ferneries,	81
Filmy Ferns,	10
Flax.	
N. Zealand,	87
Fortune's Japanese.	
jassamine,	28
palm,	29, 64
Forsythia.	
suspensa,	28
viridissima,	28
Fota,	72
Fourcroya,	77
Fremontia Californica,	87
Funkias,	52
Garrya.	
elliptica,	110
laurifolia,	110
macrophylla,	77, 110
Gazania splendens.	52
Gentians,	52
Gladiolus,	52
Gloxinias,	40
Golden Larch,	106
Griselinia.	
littoralis,	37, 44
lucida,	44
macrophylla,	37. 44, 55
Gymnogramma.	
Japonica,	34
Hakeas,	82
Heliotropa,	82
Hellebores.	
argutifolius,	48
atropurpureus.	48
atrorubens,	48
Hemlock Spruce,	103
Heterotropa asaroides,	54

	PAGE.
Himalayan Spruce,	103
Hotel Tramontano,	79
Huon Pine,	60
Hyacinths,	39, 52
Hymenophyllum,	10, 13, 16
Iberis,	52
Ilex,	42
cornuta,	42
crenata,	42
Dipyrena,	42, 83
Fortuni,	42
furcata,	42
latifolia,	43, 80, 83
Tarago,	42, 83
Imantophyllum.	
mineatum,	19, 20
Imatophyllum,	19, 20
Ipomœa,	31
Iris,	52
Iseria polycarpa,	84
Jackman's clematis,	31
Japan,	90
Japan primroses,	50
Jasminum.	
nudiflorum,	28
Jonquil,	39
Jubœa spectabilis,	29, 65, 94
Kawaka,	85
Kæmfer's Larch,	106
Lake.	
Como,	78
Maggiore,	78
Lapageria rosea,	26, 55
Levant Plane,	57
Libocedrus.	
Chilensis,	107
dolobrata,	87, 107
doniana,	85
Lycopodium,	13

Ligusticum.	
Peleponessianum,	49
Ligustrum.	
coriaceum,	36
Japonicum,	36
ovatum,	36, 58
Lilium.	
auratum,	17, 90
Canadense,	17
candidum,	17
lancifolium,	90
longifolium,	17
Neilgherrense,	17
parvum,	17
puberulum,	17
Lily of the valley,	35
Martagons,	17
Tiger lilies,	17
Limonia.	
trifoliata,	110
Lomaria.	
Chilensis,	34
Magellanica,	34
London pride,	47
Lonicera.	
Brachypoda aurea	
reticulata,	28
Fuchsioides,	28
Ledebourii,	28
Lycopodium,	13
Lythospermum prostratum,	52
fruticosum,	55
Macrozamia,	15
Magnolia.	
conspicua,	83
fuscata,	83
glauca,	83
grandiflora,	27, 83
Lennei,	83
Soulangeana,	83
Tripetala,	83
umbrella,	83
Maiden-hair tree,	108
M'Master,	86
Mandevilla suaveolens,	27
Maples,	57
Marlfield,	81
Martagon lilies,	17
Melianthus,	49
Myrtus Clequen,	47
Musas.	
Ensete,	77
Mespilus,	25
crenata,	25
Napoleon's willow,	60
Narcissus,	52
Bulbocodium,	88
conspicuus,	88
triangularis,	88
Nasturtium,	48
Negundo.	
fraxinifolium,	109
polymorphum,	109
Nertera depressa,	53
New Zealand flax,	87
Odontoglossum,	32
Oncidium,	32
Onoclea sensibilis,	34
Onychium Japonicum,	34
Oreocoma filicina,	49
Oreodaphne Californica,	86
Osmanthus,	45
Pandanus.	
utilis,	77
Veitchii,	77
Paris pride,	47
Patton's Spruce,	103
Paulownias,	57
People's gardens and parks,	75–77
Peperomia,	9
Peucedanum officinale,	49

Index.

	PAGE.
Phœnix.	
dactylifera,	15
humilis,	15
reclinata,	15
sylvestris,	15
Phalænopsis,	32
Phormium.	
Tenax variegata,	87
Piccottees,	40
Picea grandis,	84
bracteata,	84
grandis,	84
Pinus Austriaca,	105
Pinus.	
Austriaca,	105
Benthamiana,	105
Cembra,	105
excelsa,	105
Hartwegii,	105
insignis,	105
macrocarpa,	103
Pallasiana,	106
Pinsapo,	105
Pyrenaica,	105
radiata,	105
resinosa,	105
Strobus,	103
Pittosporum.	
crassifolium,	45
coreaceum,	46
Tobira,	45
Platanus.	
Occidentalis,	57
Orientalis, or digitata,	57
Podocarpus,	108
Andine,	84
Polycarpa maximowii,	84
Polysticum acrosticoides,	34
Primroses,	52
Pritchardia.	
filicina,	29
filifera,	65
Pacifica,	65

	PAGE.
Privets,	36
Prumnopytis elegans,	84
Pseudolarix,	106
Pteris.	
Cretica albo-lineata,	34
scaberula,	34
Ptychosperma Cunninghamii,	15
Pyracantha,	25
Pyrus Japonica,	25
Quercus.	
lamellosa,	111
Pannonica,	111
Ranunculi,	52
Raxopitys Cunninghamii,	107
Red, or resinous Pine,	105
Retinospora,	108
Rhaphiolepis Japonica, or ovata,	45
Rhapis flabelliformis, or flabellata,	14, 15
Rhododendrons,	36, 84
Dalhousianum,	84
Falconeri,	84
ponticum,	84
Thompsoni,	84
Richardia.	
Africana,	10, 18, 87
albo-maculata,	18
hastata,	18
Sabal.	
Andansonii,	15
umbraculifera,	15
Saccalabium,	74
Salisburia,	108
Salvias,	52
patens,	52
Saxe-Gotha conspicua,	108

Index.

	PAGE.		PAGE.
Saxifragas,	47	Thuja doniana,	85, 107
ciliata,	47	Thujopsis borealis,	108
cordifolia,	47	Tiger lilies,	17
crassifolia,	47	Todea.	
Fortuni,	47	pellucida,	12
ligulata,	47	superba,	12
Nepalensis,	47	Treculs Yucca,	35, 70
pyramidalis,	47	Trichomanes,	9, 11, 33
rosularis,	47	Trollius Asiaticus,	52
Sciadopytis,	108	Tropeolum polyphyl-	
Scillas,	20, 52	lum,	48
Seaforthia elegans,	15		
Sedums,	52	Umbrella Pine,	108
Selaginellas,	13		
Sempervivum,	52	Valotta.	
Sequoia,	108	eximea,	20
Siberian Pine,	103	major,	20
Skimmea.		purpurea,	20
fragrans,	36	Veronicas,	40, 52
Japonica,	36	Villas,	78
laureola,	36	Carlotta,	80
oblata,	36	Dr. Hudson's,	81
Sologni ocreata,	74	Farnleigh,	81
Squares, city,	41-48	Gumbleton's, Mr.	86
Statices,	52	Hay Lodge,	89
Street ornaments,	57	J. Jessop's,	81
Struthiopteris.		Lakelands, Mr.	
Germanica,	34	Crawford's,	84
Japonica,	34	Lord Gough's,	81
Pennsylvanica,	34	Mount Merrion,	81
Symphitum pictum,	52	Mr. Bagwell's,	86
		Old Conna,	82
Table ornaments,	38, 40	Riall's,	82
Tasso's Villa,	79	Roebuck Castle,	81
Taurian Pine,	105	St. Anne's,	81
Taxodium sempervirens,	108	Stawell Webb's,	82
Tea tree,	25	Tasso's,	79
Thea.		Westby's,	81
Assamica,	25	Violas,	52
Bohea,	25		
viridis,	25	Wellingtonia gigantea,	108
Thrinax.		Wistaria sinensis,	31
elegans,	15	Woodwardia radi-	
radiata,	15	cans,	34

Index.

Yuccas.	PAGE.	Yuccas—continued.	PAGE.
albo-spica.	35	recurva,	43
aloefolia,	35, 69	stricta,	35
augustifolia,	35	Treculeana.	35, 70
canaliculata.	43	variegata,	70
filamentosa.	35, 70	Whiplei,	35, 70
flaccida,	43		
gloriosa,	35, 43	Zauscherneria Cali-	
quadricolor,	70	fornica,	52

THE END.

www.ingramcontent.com/pod-product-compliance
Lightning Source LLC
Chambersburg PA
CBHW030339170426
43202CB00010B/1179